Advance Praise for
INSPIRING FORGIVENESS

"This book, masquerading as an inspirational volume, urgently points to a quality essential to our well-being. While focused on forgiveness, this is but one instance of the broader value of learning to *let go*—of our regrets, grievances, petty preoccupations, distorted and self-serving stories—all of it. Letting go of our tendency to nurture our injuries is as imperative to emotional health as it is challenging. Bonner's eloquent examples of those who have suffered more than most of us can imagine point, again and again, to the very real possibility of forgiving, and its value for us, those who have been harmed. The volume itself is lovely in its abundant use of poetry, quotes, even the typesetting. But this loveliness should not be taken to suggest the topic is trivial; indeed it points to the absolute requirement of relearning kindness toward ourselves and others as a prerequisite for restoring peace to our world."
—Paul Fulton, cofounder of the Institute for Meditation and Psychotherapy

"*Inspiring Forgiveness* is a book that has worked me into the bones of my integrity. I hate the difficulty of the process, yet love the life that holds it. This book invites a complex purifying aspect for us all—thus deepening our capacity to live together with greater freedom."
—Larry Yang, author of *Awakening Together: The Spiritual Practice of Inclusivity and Community*

"What a wonderful illumination of the power of forgiveness Barbara Bonner has given us. The book's unique gathering of personal stories, poems, and quotations shows that forgiveness is not a momentary feeling but an attitude toward life, a practice of deep self-healing, and a path to freedom. *Inspiring Forgiveness* is aptly titled, for it does more than tell us about forgiveness, it inspires us to live it."
—John Brehm, editor of *The Poetry of Impermanence, Mindfulness, and Joy*

"Forgiveness is hard won. It takes everything, and we are not in charge of the timing of the process. We have to just be completely willing. Easy to say. In this treasury, Barbara Bonner walks us through many new ways and insights to forge a new relationship to forgiveness."
—Sensei Koshin Paley Ellison, author of *Wholehearted: Slow Down, Help Out, Wake Up*

"An inspiring celebration of the greatest human virtue."
—David Loy, author of *Ecodharma: Buddhist Teachings for the Ecological Crisis*

"Bonner brings the reader into a meditative journey, discovering many facets of forgiveness along the way. A delightful read."
—Judson Brewer, MD, PhD, author of *The Craving Mind: From Cigarettes to Smartphones to Love—Why We Get Hooked and How We Can Break Bad Habits*

"*Inspiring Forgiveness* is a beautifully designed contemplation on one of the best practices we have for healing and opening our hearts."
—Elizabeth A. Stanley, PhD, author of *Widen the Window: Training Your Brain and Body to Thrive During Stress and Recover from Trauma*

"This powerful book can defuse the most destructive bombs and clean the wounds caused by the shrapnel of anger."
—Leslie Thomas, director of *The Prosecutors*

INSPIRING
FORGIVENESS

POEMS, QUOTATIONS, AND TRUE STORIES
TO HELP WITH FORGIVING
YOURSELF AND OTHERS

BARBARA BONNER

Wisdom

Wisdom Publications
199 Elm Street
Somerville, MA 02144 USA
wisdomexperience.org

*Library of Congress
Cataloging-in-Publication Data*
Names: Bonner, Barbara, 1948– author.
Title: Inspiring forgiveness: poems, quotations, and true stories to help with forgiving yourself and others / Barbara Bonner.
Description: Somerville, MA: Wisdom Publications, 2019. | Includes bibliographical references and index. |
Identifiers: LCCN 2019035420 (print) | LCCN 2019035421 (ebook) | ISBN 9781614295785 (paperback) | ISBN 9781614296027 (ebook)
Subjects: LCSH: Forgiveness.
Classification: LCC BJ1476 .B66 2019 (print) | LCC BJ1476 (ebook) | DDC 179/.9—dc23
LC record available at
https://lccn.loc.gov/2019035420
LC ebook record available at
https://lccn.loc.gov/2019035421

ISBN 978-1-61429-578-5
ebook ISBN 978-1-61429-602-7

24 23 22 21 20
5 4 3 2 1

Cover design by Amy Collier.
Interior design by Gopa & Ted 2.

HATRED NEVER CEASES
BY HATRED,
BUT BY LOVE ALONE
IS CEASED.
THIS IS AN ANCIENT
AND ETERNAL LAW.

ATTRIBUTED TO THE BUDDHA

Introduction

THIS BOOK is an invitation to stand in the light of forgiveness and feel its power to inspire you. The gift I hope to give readers is the possibility of simply resetting your compass toward forgiveness, a little at a time. No grand gesture is needed. A new perspective is no small thing, quite grand enough.

Forgiveness asks us to open our hearts to those who have wounded us, offering the chance to them and to ourselves to begin again. It is a *process*, often a slow one, of trial and error, requiring practice and great patience. Yet with even the smallest shift in how we look at the offense or the offender, our orientation can change and leave us standing in a new place, with the heavy burden of blame and grudge-holding lightened—what the mindfulness teacher Jack Kornfield calls "not carrying the hatred in your heart."

As writer and life coach Marianne Glaeser says, "Forgiving requires a counterintuitive response to the hurtful experience: relaxing clenched fists—letting go, and feeling the hurt while resisting the pull of armoring up." The effects of this shift can spread into all areas of our lives. It is this shift that can offer a path out of anger, blame, and the desire for revenge. A forgiving person creates a forgiving family and a forgiving community—and opens the possibility of a more forgiving world.

Forgiveness is an inner activity of the heart. Forgetting is not required, nor is action, nor apology. No one needs to know that it has occurred. Sometimes we succeed and

"I learned a long time ago

that some people would rather die than forgive.

It's a strange truth, but forgiveness is a painful

and difficult process. It's not something that

happens overnight. It's an evolution of the heart."

SUE MONK KIDD

sometimes we fail, but we can always hold forgiveness as an intention. Forgiveness cannot be forced. We can create the conditions likely to encourage its growth, but we cannot will it into existence. It is something we usually have to ponder long and hard. For a few lucky ones, it arises spontaneously. It can be a radical act, often quite bold. There is rarely applause. Those closest to us may disapprove or disagree with our new perspective. It can be risky. It is rarely necessary. We often feel no compelling, outward pressure to forgive. This is an act we do for ourselves. It is also how we lift each other up. It is a way to fight cynicism and retain our hopes and dreams. It is a radical act of love. Robert Enright, founder of the International Forgiveness Institute, describes it as "loving gentleness toward those who are stoning us."

In forgiving, we often have to live within the world of mysteries and doubts, let go of the self as the ultimate point of reference, relinquish the sovereignty of the ego. Forgiveness is rarely a linear, logical act. It often requires a leap. Likewise, being able to forgive forces us to give up our need for absolutes. We tend to like black and white, true and false, good and evil; forgiveness forces us into the territory of grays.

FORGIVENESS AND RELIGION

Forgiveness plays a central role in all the world's major religions. I have interviewed rabbis, Christian ministers, Muslim scholars, and some of the great Buddhist teachers of our contemporary world. I include a story in this book on Amish forgiveness. We can witness the central role of forgiveness in the deeply moving services for Yom Kippur, and the Torah explicitly forbids us to take revenge or bear grudges. In Christianity, confession of sins opens a door to forgiveness and moving on. Devout Muslims pray for forgiveness five times a day and see it as "a state of the heart that is to be aspired to and regularly practiced through prayer, fasting, charity, self-cultivation and kindness," according to the Islamic scholar Celene Ibrahim.

My own understanding of forgiveness is especially informed by my many years of Buddhist study and practice, including long retreats with great teachers. Just as with my work on generosity and courage in my two previous books, I believe that true forgiveness is a natural outgrowth of a life lived on the Eightfold Path. Forgiveness comes from a mind that does not cling. In many ways, non-clinging is the essence of freedom. When we are present to a painful experience and cultivate curiosity towards it, a natural compassion can arise that makes forgiveness possible. Compassion lies at the very heart of forgiveness.

In her book *Real Love*, meditation teacher Sharon Salzberg urges us to allow ourselves to wrestle with anger and pain as a first step to forgiveness. "We can then invite ourselves to consider alternative modes of viewing our pain and can see that releasing our grip on anger and resentment can actually be an act of self-compassion," she writes. The fifth-century Buddhist teacher Buddhaghosa compared harboring anger and resentment to holding a burning ember in our hand in order to hurl at an enemy—only to realize that we are the one getting burned.

THE SCIENCE OF FORGIVENESS

In recent years, forgiveness has been the focus of a wave of scientific study, confirming the unsurprising finding that to forgive is actually good for our physical and mental health. It can lower blood pressure, help us deal with stress more effectively, and keep depression at bay. It offers benefits to the cardiovascular and immune systems.

But if it is so good for us, why is forgiveness so hard to embrace for so many of us?

In his book *Forgive for Good*, Fred Luskin, head of Stanford University's Forgiveness Project, offers a scientific perspective: "We are hardwired to remember pain and loss. Our brains are designed to maximize remembrance of suffering so one can be alert in case it happens again." To counter this inclination, studies in evolution point to the necessity of cooperation to our survival. Individuals and cultures that are able to work together survive and prosper. And we all know just how often we need to overlook, even forgive, slights and insults in order to cooperate. It's a tall order. Forgiveness is a decision for which we must each find our own individual motivation.

In Western culture, forgiveness is not highly valued and is rarely taught. Michael McCullough, director of the Evolution and Human Behavior Laboratory at the University of Miami and author of *On Revenge*, assesses how revenge came to have a purpose in human life: "Human beings are more instinctively equipped for forgiveness than we've perhaps given ourselves credit for. Knowing this suggests ways to calm the revenge instinct in ourselves and others and embolden the forgiveness intuition." He believes that the desire for revenge "does not come from some sick, dark part of how our minds operate. It is a craving to solve a problem and accomplish a goal"—one of the most generous views I have found of the desire for revenge.

THE INVITATION

In my first two books, *Inspiring Generosity* and *Inspiring Courage*, I wrote about "lightning bolt" moments of sudden inspiration that can change us profoundly in just an instant. My hope in this book is to offer a modest but potent reconsideration of forgiveness in our individual and collective lives, and an opportunity to pause and consider what role you want to offer forgiveness in your own life.

"If you are trying to forgive; even if you manage forgiving in fits and starts, if you forgive today, hate again tomorrow, and have to forgive again the day after, you are a forgiver. Most of us are amateurs . . . So what? In this game, nobody is an expert. We are all beginners."

LEWIS B. SMEDES

Even a first step in the direction of forgiveness—just 10 percent more—changes our internal landscape. Were the world at large to move in that direction, it would change our communities, systems, governments, policies, and international relations. Just as we all have engaged in regrettable actions at points in our lives, so too have nations committed acts of hatred and aggression that have led to further acts of vengeance and, ultimately, world wars. Imagine for a moment what might ensue if the nations of the world could embrace a 10 percent shift toward forgiveness.

This book does not offer answers or recipes for forgiveness; rather, it poses what I think are the important questions, and presents the wise words of philosophers, writers, poets, and great thinkers from across centuries and continents, which can serve as guideposts along the path to bringing greater forgiveness into our lives. My hope is that each and every reader will find here a moment of reflection—whether in the briefest of quotations, a poem, or the story of someone whose life was forever changed by forgiveness.

Buddhist teacher Pema Chödrön offers this simple practice for cultivating forgiveness: "First we acknowledge what we feel—shame, revenge, embarrassment, remorse. Then we forgive ourselves for being human. Then, in the spirit of not wallowing in the pain, we let go and make a fresh start. We don't have to carry the burden with us anymore. We will discover forgiveness as a natural expression of the open heart, an expression of our basic goodness. This potential is inherent in every moment. Each moment is an opportunity to make a fresh start."

This book is a collection of those moments.

For those struggling with either offering or asking for forgiveness, I hope this book offers inspiration. I hope friends will give it to friends engaged in this struggle. And, for those who cannot bring themselves to ask for forgiveness, perhaps giving this book as a gift may open new pathways. May it speak for you before you can utter the words.

MY PATH TO FORGIVENESS

In writing this book, I was completely unprepared for how immersion in the material would change my own life. Early on, I was able to confront two situations in which I had let down people who had been close to me. These offenses, though relatively minor, had lived with me for many years, festering and gnawing. I decided to write both of these people a letter of apology. I asked for nothing. I simply wanted to express how much they had meant to me, and how I regretted my own behavior and any hurt it had caused. One wrote back somewhat glibly and suspiciously, and the other very lovingly. To some extent, the responses mattered far less than what I was able to put into words. It brought home to me the extent to which forgiveness can be a very quiet, even intimate, activity. There is no drum roll, and we may never receive a grateful response, or any response at all.

I am fortunate to have only rarely suffered intense personal pain. For me, forgiveness has focused largely on an examination of my inner life. But I have always been an engaged spectator of the pain of the world, and of the way that pain can be eased by forgiving hearts.

Like most families, mine has not escaped its share of dysfunction. One particularly painful episode lived with me for years until I felt its grip on me ease, inch by inch, over the course of a decade and continuing to this day. It was a visceral experience of forgiveness as a process. Sometimes we can only forgive a little, then rest there until, perhaps, another small space opens up into which we can move forward. After a long, sometimes very hard slog, the sun might begin to show itself. At least it did for me. If a leap of forgiveness is not available to you, I urge you to tackle forgiveness in baby steps.

"If you let go a little,

you will have a little happiness.

If you let go a lot,

you will have a lot of happiness.

If you let go completely,

you will be free."

AJAHN CHAH

Life is *dukkha*—a Buddhist concept commonly translated as "suffering." To live is to be hurt, slighted, dismissed, harmed. We always stand at a crossroads—with the choice of accumulating grievances, which color our future in painful ways, or acknowledging them and not letting them stick to us.

THE BOOK'S OFFERINGS

I hope you will be as moved as I have been by the stories I recount here of a dozen extraordinary people who shared the powerful impact of forgiveness in their own lives. Each is markedly different from the others. In every story, it is the life lived in forgiveness that I wish to spotlight far more than the individual acts. Alongside their experiences, I offer you the words of 40 poets who see forgiveness through 40 different lenses; and more than 100 inspiring quotations from some of our world's great thinkers, teachers, religious leaders, philosophers, artists, and writers. Fortunately for us, many of them also believe in the power of humor!

Some stories may seem extreme. Sometimes forgiveness can appear unfathomable, unreachable, even just plain wrong. I ask you to step into each subject's shoes, to try to feel what they felt, and to imagine bringing forgiveness to the situation as if it were your life. Just *trying* may change you. Simply observing and considering have value. Years from now, in an especially challenging situation, you may recall that person's story and the forgiveness they were able to bring forth.

First among stories of forgiveness is that of the Dalai Lama, the great world leader whose daily meditations focus on the healing power of forgiveness for the human family. With every reason to hold anger and a wish for vengeance against those who invaded his country and ravaged its Buddhist culture, he instead chooses compassion and forgiveness.

A hero to me and to many, Congressman John Lewis of Georgia is often referred to as "the conscience of the Congress." From his earliest days of activism for civil rights, the power of forgiveness was always a light by which he steered. In his story, we see how forgiveness was central not only to his own life but also to that of the entire civil rights movement.

When young American Fulbright student Amy Biehl was killed in mob violence in the final days of apartheid in South Africa, her devastated family would have been justified in turning to bitterness and hatred. Instead, they forged bonds with Amy's African friends, colleagues, and even her killers to establish a foundation that would further their daughter's work. Their story stretches the very definition of forgiveness, especially for any parent who has lost a child.

Many of us may remember hearing of the 2006 shootings of 10 young students in a one-room schoolhouse in the Amish country of Pennsylvania. The ways in which this deeply religious community reacted to the death of five girls and serious wounding of five others offers a window into the power of forgiveness when it is taught as a part of daily life, from a child's earliest years. In the story of a community defined by forgiveness, there are important lessons for our larger society, nation, and world.

The story of Eva Mozes Kor, victim of the cruel Nazi doctor Josef Mengele during her imprisonment at Auschwitz, stretches all bounds of what we consider possible as we contemplate our own ability to forgive. Some will be appalled by her story, others inspired. But it is an important story to tell as we test what we consider our own outer limits of forgiveness.

What started as an ordinary day in the London life of design professional Gill Hicks turned into unimaginable horror as she became the victim of a subway bomber. As she recovered, she—like many of those featured here—had the choice of allowing the irreparable damage to her body and to her life to move her toward hate, or toward forgiveness and reconciliation.

I tell the gripping story of Immaculée Ilibagiza, a young Rwandan university student suddenly forced into hiding when brutal tribal massacres overtook her country. Most of her family was murdered while she spent 90 days hiding in a tiny bathroom in her pastor's house with seven other women. She attributes her embrace of forgiveness to both her survival and what she later managed to create in her new life.

Many of our hearts broke with the news of the murders, in June 2015, of the Charleston clergy and church members now known as the Emmanuel Nine. What inspired the families of the victims to forgive such a heinous crime? Their stories tell us how and why they chose forgiveness.

Will Morales, now Commissioner of Boston Centers for Youth and Families, grew up in a world of hatred, street violence, and crime. At a critical juncture in his life, he was offered a helping hand that became the key to his creation of a new life with forgiveness at its core. Will's story brings home our power in each moment to change another's life with kindness and compassion.

My friend Sue Klebold, whom I have known since childhood, will likely always be known as the mother of Columbine killer Dylan Klebold. One fateful day, with utterly no inkling of what was about to happen, she learned that her son had murdered 12 students and one teacher, and wounded another 20 before taking his own life. What do we do in moments in which everything comes crashing down? Sue's challenge is centered on the hard work of self-forgiveness.

"Finish each day and be done with it.

You have done what you could. Some blunders and absurdities

have crept in; forget them as soon as you can. Tomorrow is

a new day. You shall begin it serenely with too high a spirit

to be encumbered with your old nonsense."

RALPH WALDO EMERSON

Wesley Clark Jr., a lieutenant in the US Army and the son of the retired NATO commander, served our country with unquestioned loyalty. But a trip to the protests at the Standing Rock Sioux Reservation in 2016 opened his heart to the ways in which this nation needs to seek forgiveness for its many crimes against indigenous populations. His account of a forgiveness ceremony that he and a group of veterans performed with elders of the Sioux tribe is a moving testimony to the power of forgiveness.

Two much-beloved Buddhist monks who work with the dying shed light on how forgiveness can assume a central role when our days are numbered. Koshin Paley Ellison and Robert Chodo Campbell tell of the many unexpected forms and disguises that forgiveness can take in these crucial days.

Each section of this book begins with one of these stories, and is accompanied by poems and quotations that support and enhance its theme. You might want to read it straight through, or dip in, savoring one section at a time. I hope you will discover words and stories that resonate deeply with you, and that they will serve as inspiration as you continue to explore the power of forgiveness in your own life.

"FORGIVENESS IS ABOUT HEALING SUFFERING FOR
OURSELVES AND OTHERS. UNTIL WE DEVELOP COMPASSION
WITHIN OURSELVES AND A CONCERN ABOUT THE
WELFARE OF OTHERS, WE CANNOT TRULY FORGIVE."

HIS HOLINESS THE DALAI LAMA

His Holiness the Dalai Lama

IN CONSIDERING individuals whose lives offer inspiring examples of forgiveness, it is
hard to imagine a better place to begin than with a deep bow to His Holiness the
Dalai Lama.

This towering figure of compassion not only deliberately brings what he calls "the
unrelenting pursuit of forgiveness" into each waking hour, but also makes what can
seem an impossibly lofty goal appear fully accessible.

Despite the demands of a superhuman schedule, His Holiness arises each morning
at 3:30 to begin his day with several hours of formal meditation. "All major religious
traditions carry basically the same message," he says, "that is love, compassion and
forgiveness . . . the important thing is they should be part of our daily lives." A core
focus in these hours is the understanding that we are all intricately related as human

beings, regardless of geographical, political, ethnic, gender, or religious differences. We all struggle for the same happiness and release from unhappiness. But to hold this truth in our minds takes devoted, unceasing attention.

In a worldview that acknowledges the interconnectedness of all beings, the Dalai Lama finds no room for the concept of "enemy." As he says, "Destruction of your neighbor as enemy is essentially destruction of yourself." Rage against others makes it impossible for us to absorb the often-hidden lessons they offer. His Holiness regards his "enemies" as his most valuable teachers, as they provide the challenge to continually cultivate and sharpen his capacity for forgiveness and compassion. "In my experience, the period of greatest gain in knowledge and experience is the most difficult period in one's life," he has said. "Through a difficult period, you can learn, you can develop inner strength, determination, and courage to face the problem. Who gives you this chance? Your enemy."

His Holiness reminds us that, in contemplating forgiveness, it is important to distinguish between the act and the actor. A sin can lie beyond forgiveness, but we can always hold out a shred of hope for the sinner. Often criticized for not advocating revenge against the Chinese for their crimes against the Tibetan people, he sees such a notion as completely foreign to his nature: "They've already taken my country. Why should I let them have my mind, too?"

His Holiness frequently illustrates his teachings on forgiveness with the story of Lopon Tenzin Namdak Rinpoche, a Tibetan monk who was imprisoned and brutally tortured by the Chinese for 18 years before escaping to India. In his early conversations with the monk, the Dalai Lama asked him if he had ever been afraid during his long ordeal. Without hesitation, Lupon-la responded that he had only feared losing his compassion for his Chinese captors. The Dalai Lama is convinced that this monk

FORGIVENESS
IS THE ONLY WAY
TO REVERSE THE
IRREVERSIBLE FLOW
OF HISTORY.

HANNAH ARENDT

"I think the reason that remarkable stories

of forgiveness take our breath away is that we instantly feel

the liberation in the lifting of boundaries, the end of separation,

of *inside* and *outside*."

NANCY MUJO BAKER

survived only because he embraced forgiveness so wholeheartedly. His Holiness sees suffering and adversity as necessary preconditions for developing patience, tolerance, and forgiveness.

When told the story of a young Tibetan boy who was brutally tortured by Chinese soldiers, the Dalai Lama acknowledged the natural human reaction of anger while, at the same time, invoking the power of its antidote. "First I was angry, then I felt sorry for the officer . . . You can't blame that person. Under circumstances like that, even I myself may act like that. So, thinking along this line, instead of anger, forgiveness and compassion come."

His Holiness embraces the revolutionary concept that "to forgive is actually the best form of self-interest." But this is an enlightened self-interest in which one's own peace of mind, free from anger and vindictiveness, builds on itself, amplifying its power for goodness. "When other beings, especially those who hold a grudge against you, abuse and harm you out of envy, you should not abandon them, but hold them as objects of your greatest compassion and take care of them."

The Dalai Lama's teachings open pathways to acknowledging and embracing feelings of anger in order to move through them to an acceptance of our shared humanity and the desire for forgiveness that flows from it. In his words: "Forgiveness means you shouldn't develop feeling of revenge. Because revenge harms the other person, therefore it is a form of violence. With violence, there is usually counter-violence. This generates even more violence—the problem never goes away. So that is one level. Another level: forgiveness means you should try not to develop feelings of anger toward your enemy. Anger doesn't solve the problem. Anger only brings uncomfortable feelings toward yourself. Anger destroys your own peace of mind."

In a world awash in anger, violence, and vindictiveness, it is no small task that the Dalai Lama has set for us. Yet it is a challenge so many have risen to meet, with life-changing results—results that feed both their own "self-interest" and the well-being of all those whose lives they touch.

LOVE

YOUR CROOKED NEIGHBOR
WITH YOUR OWN
CROOKED HEART.

W. H. AUDEN

"'I can forgive, but I cannot forget'

is only another way of saying, 'I will not forgive.'

Forgiveness ought to be like a canceled note—torn in two

and burned up so that it never can be shown against one."

HENRY WARD BEECHER

ANCESTRY

My DNA results came back.

Just as I suspected, my great great grandfather

was a monarch butterfly.

Much of who I am is still wriggling under a stone.

I am part larva, but part hummingbird too.

There is dinosaur tar in my bone marrow.

My golden hair sprang out of a meadow in Palestine.

Genghis Khan is my fourth cousin,

but I didn't get his dimples.

My loins are loaded with banyan seeds from Sri Lanka,

but I descended from Ravanna, not Ram.

My uncle is a mastodon.

There are traces of white people in my saliva.

3.7 billion years ago I swirled in the golden dust,

dreaming of a planet overgrown with lingams and yonis.

More recently, say 60,000 B.C.

I walked on hairy paws across a land bridge

joining Sweden to Botswana.

I am the bastard of the sun and moon.

I can no longer hide my heritage of raindrops and cougar scat.

My mud was molded with your grandmother's tears.

I am the brother from a rival tribe

who marched you to the sea and sold you.

I am the merchant from Savannah, and the cargo of blackness.

I am the chain.

Admit it, you have wings, vast and crystal,

like mine, like mine.

You have sweat, dark and salty,

like mine, like mine.

You have secrets silently singing in your blood,

like mine, like mine.

Don't pretend that earth is not one family.

Don't pretend we never hung from the same branch.

Don't pretend we don't ripen on each other's breath.

Don't pretend we didn't come here to forgive.

FRED LaMOTTE

IF WE HAVE

NO PEACE,

IT'S BECAUSE

WE'VE **FORGOTTEN**

WE BELONG TO

EACH OTHER.

MOTHER TERESA

FORGIVENESS
WILL CHANGE
YOUR LIFE
AND CHANGE
OUR WORLD.

DESMOND TUTU

"Einstein's $E = mc^2$ is an extraordinary concept.

So radical; matter and energy are two phases of the same sort

of general stuff. There's only one other idea that radical: Forgive us

our trespasses as we forgive those who trespass against us."

KURT VONNEGUT

A POISON TREE

I was angry with my friend;
I told my wrath, my wrath did end.
I was angry with my foe:
I told it not, my wrath did grow.

And I water'd it in fears,
Night & morning with my tears:
And I sunned it with smiles,
And with soft deceitful wiles.

And it grew both day and night.
Till it bore an apple bright.
And my foe beheld it shine,
And he knew that it was mine.

And into my garden stole,
When the night had veil'd the pole;
In the morning glad I see;
My foe outstretched beneath the tree.

WILLIAM BLAKE

> "NONVIOLENCE AND FORGIVENESS ARE NOT
> JUST AN IDEA, BUT A WAY OF LIFE FOR ME."
>
> CONGRESSMAN JOHN LEWIS

Congressman John Lewis

THE QUALITIES of forgiveness and committed activism are rarely seen as interwoven. But for Congressman John Lewis, "the capacity to forgive and move toward reconciliation," has been at the heart of both the civil rights movement and his own life.

The great civil rights leader, known for decades as "the conscience of the Congress," was born in 1940 in Troy, Alabama, to Willie Mae and Eddie Lewis. One of ten children, this child of sharecroppers grew up in deeply segregated Pike County. Schools were segregated; the local library had a "No Coloreds" sign. Lewis remembers seeing only two white people before the age of six.

Life changed for Lewis when he went to Nashville to study, first at the Baptist Theological Seminary and later at Fisk University. An early trip to Buffalo, New York, gave him a life-changing, close-up view of integration. In his college years, Lewis became active in nonviolent protests in Nashville to desegregate lunch counters. His life as a

FORGIVENESS IS THE KEY TO ACTION AND FREEDOM.

HANNAH ARENDT

young activist led him to meetings with Rosa Parks in 1957, and a deep friendship with Martin Luther King Jr.

In 1960, Lewis became one of the original Freedom Riders—groups of black and white activists committing the then-illegal act of riding together by bus from Washington to New Orleans. During this time of nonviolent activism, he was the victim of multiple attacks and injuries, and was arrested and jailed 24 times by 1963.

As chair of the Student Nonviolent Coordinating Committee, Lewis was one of the "Big Six" civil rights leaders who led the 1963 march on Washington. But he may be best remembered for the event known as Bloody Sunday, on March 7, 1965, when he and Hosea Williams were met with brutal beatings, arrests, and violence as they attempted to peacefully lead 600 marchers across the Edmund Pettus Bridge in Selma. Lewis commemorates that day by making an annual pilgrimage to Alabama to retrace the march—now accompanied by dignitaries from government and every area of civic life, who regularly vie for the chance to go on this historic journey with him.

As today's most distinguished living link to the early years of the civil rights movement, Lewis continues to speak out on important issues relating to justice and human rights—from voting rights, to gun safety, to immigration reform and the Dreamers Act. Each year between 1988 and 1993, he introduced a bill in Congress to establish a national African-American museum, an effort that finally led to the 2016 opening of the National Museum of African American History and Culture on the Mall in Washington. Throughout these years of committed activism, Lewis has been spurred to action by his dream of what he calls (following Dr. King) "the Beloved Community" in America.

Two examples of Lewis' forgiveness in action are particularly illustrative of his philosophy.

There have been few more ardent segregationists in our country's political life than

George Wallace, former governor of Alabama and presidential candidate, whose mantra was "Segregation now, segregation tomorrow, segregation forever." His cruel rhetoric created a pervasive atmosphere of hate and violence. But when Lewis and Wallace met for the first time in 1979, Lewis was struck by the realization that Wallace's heart had undergone a sea change. He seemed to be actively seeking forgiveness from the African Americans he had oppressed, taking ownership of his earlier bigotry. Lewis concluded, "When I met George Wallace, I had to forgive him, because to do otherwise—to hate him—would only perpetuate the evil system we sought to destroy."

He continues: "George Wallace should be remembered for his capacity to change. And we are better as a nation because of our capacity to forgive and to acknowledge that our political leaders are human and largely a reflection of the social currents in the river of history. . . . I can never forget what George Wallace said and did as governor, as a national leader and as a political opportunist. But our ability to forgive serves a higher moral purpose in our society. Through genuine repentance and forgiveness, the soul of our nation is redeemed. George Wallace deserves to be remembered for his effort to redeem his soul and in so doing to mend the fabric of American society."

John Lewis fully embodies the truth Dr. King famously named: "Hate is too heavy a burden to bear." And, like Dr. King, John Lewis decided to stick to love.

Another example: In 1961, Lewis, Albert Bigelow (who was white), and a group of Freedom Riders arrived at a Greyhound Bus Terminal in Rock Hill, South Carolina, and attempted to enter a waiting room designated "for whites only." The two leaders were brutally beaten by a group of five young white men. True to their principles of nonviolence, Lewis and Bigelow neither fought back nor pressed charges.

One of the attackers, Elwin Wilson, silently carried the burden of guilt for that assault until 2009, when Obama's election caused a moment of awakening for him. He called

"He that cannot forgive others

breaks the bridge over which he must pass himself,

for every man has need to be forgiven."

LORD EDWARD HERBERT

his local paper in an attempt to learn the identity of his victim as a first step to making amends. Armed with the shocking new knowledge that the distinguished Congressman was the one he had attacked over 45 years earlier, Elwin traveled to Washington with his son to beg for Lewis's forgiveness. In a poignant, tear-filled meeting in the Congressional office, Wilson apologized, then asked for and received Lewis's unhesitating forgiveness. Lewis summed up the moment and the lifetime of devoted work that led up to it: "I never thought this would happen. . . It says something about the power of love, of grace, the power of the people being able to say 'I'm sorry' and move on."

INJURIES
TOO WELL REMEMBERED
CANNOT HEAL.

BENJAMIN BARBER

THERE'S NO POINT
IN BURYING THE HATCHET
IF YOU'RE GOING TO PUT
A MARKER ON THE SITE.

SYDNEY HARRIS

A TOTAL STRANGER ONE BLACK DAY

a total stranger one black day
knocked living the hell out of me—

who found forgiveness hard because
my(as it happened)self he was

-but now that fiend and i are such
immortal friends the other's each.

E. E. CUMMINGS

"We must develop and maintain the capacity to forgive. He who is devoid of the power to forgive is devoid of the power to love. There is some good in the worst of us and some evil in the best of us. When we discover this, we are less prone to hate our enemies."

MARTIN LUTHER KING JR.

THE CURE AT TROY *(excerpt)*

Human beings suffer
They torture one another,
They get hurt and get hard.
No poem or play or song
Can fully right a wrong
Inflicted and endured.

The innocent in gaols
Beat on their bars together.
A hunger-striker's father
Stands in the graveyard dumb.
The police widow in veils
Faints at the funeral home.

History says, *Don't hope*
On this side of the grave . . .
But then, once in a lifetime
The longed-for tidal wave

Of justice can rise up,

And hope and history rhyme.

So hope for a great sea-change

On the far side of revenge.

Believe that a further shore

Is reachable from here.

Believe in miracles

And cures and healing wells.

Call miracle self-healing:

The utter, self-revealing

Double-take of feeling.

If there's fire on the mountain

Or lightning and storm

And a god speaks from the sky

That means someone is hearing

The outcry and the birth-cry

Of new life at its term.

SÉAMUS HEANEY

"One who takes vengeance or bears a grudge

acts like one who, having cut one hand while handling a knife,

avenges himself by stabbing the other hand."

JERUSALEM TALMUD, NEDARIM 9.4

"Forgiving is not forgetting;

it's actually remembering—remembering and not using

your right to hit back. It's a second chance for a new beginning.

And the remembering part is particularly important.

Especially if you don't want to repeat what happened."

DESMOND TUTU

FORGIVENESS
IS THE FRAGRANCE
THAT THE VIOLET
SHEDS ON THE HEEL
THAT HAS CRUSHED IT.

MARK TWAIN

A PRAYER FOR RECONCILIATION

Where there is separation,
there is pain.
And where there is pain,
there is story.

And where there is story,
there is understanding,
and misunderstanding,
listening
and not listening.

May we—separated peoples,
    estranged strangers,
unfriended families, divided
    communities—
turn toward each other,

and turn toward our stories,
with understanding
and listening,
with argument and acceptance,
with challenge, change
and consolation.

Because if God is to be found,
God will be found
in the space
between.

Amen.

PÁDRAIG Ó TUAMA

The Family of Amy Biehl

DURING THE SUMMER of 1993, South Africa was approaching the end of a long road in its painful struggle for democracy. After serving 27 years in prison for his anti-apartheid activism, Nelson Mandela had been released in February 1990, and his voice was stronger than ever. Archbishop Desmond Tutu, who had won the Nobel Peace Prize in 1984, was universally hailed as a spiritual leader for this challenging time. Both men were actively working toward a peaceful transition to a democratic government, and both acknowledged that forgiveness had a tremendous role to play after the death of more than 16,000 people.

Though on the horizon, peace was far from assured, as widespread violence erupted that year. The country's long history of oppression and tyranny was hard to dislodge, and those who had suffered the most were losing patience and turning to violent action. On

"Forgiveness is a heartache and difficult to achieve because strangely, the act of forgiveness not only refuses to eliminate the original wound, but actually draws us closer to its source. To approach forgiveness is to close in on the nature of the hurt itself, the only remedy being, as we approach its raw center, to reimagine our relation to it."

DAVID WHYTE

July 25, black gunmen burst into an evening service for a thousand white worshippers at St. James Church in a white suburb of Cape Town, killing 11 and injuring 58 more. The black townships around Cape Town were no longer deemed safe for even the most peace-loving whites.

It was in this time of both hope and tragedy that 26-year-old Amy Biehl, a white American and recent Stanford graduate, elected to spend her Fulbright year studying and actively working for the cause of women's rights in the unfolding democracy. Since early childhood, Amy had been fascinated by Africa. In her post-graduate years in Washington, she had worked for the National Democratic Institute for African Affairs and traveled extensively to Namibia and other African nations. But her most passionate interest had always been focused on South Africa, and now she had been selected for the honor of an award that would allow her to be living and studying there in this pivotal year in its history.

Always a conscientious and passionate student, Amy threw herself into her work, choosing to study at the largely black University of the Western Cape rather than the predominantly white University of Cape Town. Colleagues were in awe of her accomplishments after just two months. She quickly learned to speak Xhosa. She established herself as a senior researcher at UWC, formed key relationships with the women's organizations in the area, and earned high praise from leading academics and activists. She was readily accepted by black South Africans, while many of her white colleagues struggled to make connections.

On August 25, two days before her scheduled return to the United States, Amy gave three black friends a ride into the township of Gugulethu, an area that had experienced recent mob violence against whites. She had been warned to stay away, but she was so at home in the area, and the prospect of a short drive with local friends seemed safe enough. Amy often said that she always felt safe in South Africa, no matter the circumstances. But this night, her luck ran out. A mob of black youths chanting anti-apartheid slogans stoned first her car and then her body as she attempted to escape. As she lay on the ground near her car, she was knifed in the heart by one of the young men, and died while waiting for an ambulance to arrive.

Many acknowledged that the sole reason for her being stabbed was that she was white. In her immersion in the culture, she had nearly forgotten her whiteness in the eyes of others. As the South Africa–based *New York Times* writer Barry Bearak later wrote, when "impromptu mob justice" takes hold, an apprehended person "becomes the sacrificial culprit for a thousand grievances."

At home in California, Amy's parents, Linda and Peter Biehl, reeled at the news of their daughter's death. They experienced the shock and bottomless pain of those who lose a child. But even initially they did not experience the anger to which they were, arguably, entitled. Linda's quiet prayer in those first moments was for forgiveness for her daughter's killers. As Peter was later to remark, "We have come to realize that there is no logical sense for bitterness or anger."

Few had known the extent of Amy's impact until her death. The outpouring of love and admiration for her and sadness at her loss were a testament to the spirit with which she had infused her life and work. She was hailed as a hero by both Nelson Mandela and Archbishop Tutu. Linda and Peter received condolences from President Clinton, Coretta Scott King, and hundreds of Amy's friends and colleagues. Three South African students flew to Amy's memorial service in California.

Less than six weeks after her killing, the Biehls visited South Africa as a tribute to their daughter. They met her friends and colleagues, and learned all they could about her work and its impact. In the ensuing years, they made many trips to Cape Town as

TRUE FORGIVENESS DEALS WITH THE PAST, ALL OF THE PAST, TO MAKE THE FUTURE POSSIBLE.

DESMOND TUTU

FORGIVENESS

My heart was heavy, for its trust had been
Abused, its kindness answered with foul wrong;
So, turning gloomily from my fellow-men,
One summer Sabbath day I strolled among
The green mounds of the village burial-place;
Where, pondering how all human love and hate
Find one sad level; and how, soon or late,
Wronged and wrongdoer, each with meekened face,
And cold hands folded over a still heart,
Pass the green threshold of our common grave,
Whither all footsteps tend, whence none depart,
Awed for myself, and pitying my race,
Our common sorrow, like a mighty wave,
Swept all my pride away, and trembling I forgave!

JOHN GREENLEAF WHITTIER

they considered how to give form to their growing commitment to forgiveness. They attended the trial of the four young men accused of Amy's murder, hearing all the gruesome details of her death and somehow always managing to hold onto the spirit of forgiveness for the young men and sympathy for their families.

After her killers were sentenced to eighteen years in prison, they went before the Truth and Reconciliation Committee, headed by Archbishop Tutu and formed in the belief that South Africans would have to learn to forgive past conflicts in order to move forward. There the Biehls supported amnesty for the young men. As Peter remarked over and over, "It is liberating to forgive. . . Forgiveness reestablished their humanity and gave them a second chance."

For the Biehls, the journey to become the "icons of forgiveness" that they were later called was often very challenging. But the spirit of forgiveness had become part of the South African culture. At Mandela's inauguration, eight months after Amy's death, the new leader invited his former jailer to attend and sit in the VIP section.

In 1994, the Biehls established the Amy Biehl Foundation to honor and continue their daughter's work. After a few years, they decided that the ultimate act of forgiveness would be hiring Easy Nofemela and Ntobeko Peni, two of Amy's killers, as employees of the foundation. "We hope the spirits of Amy and those like her will be a force in their new lives," they said. "Amy was drawn to South Africa as a student and she admired the vision of Nelson Mandela of a Rainbow Nation. It is this vision of forgiveness and reconciliation that we have honored." After Peter's death in 2002, Linda has continued the foundation's humanitarian work in the black townships of the region.

Amy embodied the African spirit of *ubuntu*—the sense of shared humanity and inter-connectedness among all humankind. Linda Biehl fully embraces this spirit in the focus of the foundation's ongoing work: "When you shake someone's hand—even though they might have harmed you—you feel their touch, you look into their eyes. You say *you're a human being, just like me.* It melts away the layers and gets to the essence of what we are underneath . . . just people, with all the same wants and needs and emotions. Amy's death put us on a path to realize that."

"'He abused me, he struck me,

he overpowered me, he robbed me.'

Those who harbor such thoughts do not still their hatred.

'He abused me, he struck me, he overpowered me, he robbed me.'

Those who do not harbor such thoughts still their hatred."

BUDDHA, *THE DHAMMAPADA*

PRAYER BEFORE THE PRAYER

I want to be willing to forgive

But I dare not ask for the will to forgive

In case you give it to me

And I am not yet ready

I am not yet ready for my heart to soften

I am not yet ready to be vulnerable again

Not yet ready to see that there is humanity in my tormentor's eyes

Or that the one who hurt me may also have cried

I am not yet ready for the journey

I am not yet interested in the path

I am at the prayer before the prayer of forgiveness

Grant me the will to want to forgive

Grant it to me not yet but soon

Can I even form the words

Forgive me?

Dare I even look?

Do I dare to see the hurt I have caused?

I can glimpse all the shattered pieces of that fragile thing

That soul trying to rise on the broken wings of hope

But only out of the corner of my eye

I am afraid of it

And if I am afraid to see

How can I not be afraid to say

Forgive me?

Is there a place where we can meet?

You and me

The place in the middle

Where we straddle the lines

Where you are right

And I am right too

And both of us are wrong and wronged

Can we meet there?

And look for the place where the path begins

The path that ends when we forgive.

DESMOND TUTU AND MPHO TUTU

IF WE REALLY WANT To LOVE WE MUST LEARN HOW To FORGIVE.

MOTHER TERESA

"When we manage a flash of mercy

for someone we don't like, especially a truly awful person,

including ourselves, we experience a great spiritual

moment, a new point of view that can make us gasp."

ANNE LAMOTT

"You will learn a lot from yourself

if you stretch in the direction of goodness, of bigness,

of kindness, of forgiveness, or emotional bravery.

Be a warrior for love."

CHERYL STRAYED

SONNET CXX

That you were once unkind befriends me now,

And for that sorrow, which I then did feel,

Needs must I under my transgression bow,

Unless my nerves were brass or hammered steel.

For if you were by my unkindness shaken,

As I by yours, you've passed a hell of time;

And I, a tyrant, have no leisure taken

To weigh how once I suffered in your crime.

O! that our night of woe might have remembered

My deepest sense, how hard true sorrow hits,

And soon to you, as you to me, then tendered

The humble salve, which wounded bosoms fits!

    But that your trespass now becomes a fee;

    Mine ransoms yours, and yours must ransom me.

WILLIAM SHAKESPEARE

Amish Forgiveness

THE BEAUTIFUL FARM land of Lancaster County, Pennsylvania, is home to about 30,000 members of the Amish community, a Pennsylvania Dutch subculture dating back to the sixteenth century that combines devout Christian faith with an austerely simple lifestyle. As part of their commitment to living outside mainstream contemporary culture, the Amish choose to educate their children separately in the approximately 190 schoolhouses they have built in the county over the years.

On the morning of October 2, 2006, Charles Roberts, a local man who had always lived in close proximity and on friendly terms with his Amish neighbors, burst into the one-room schoolhouse at Nickel Mines, just south of Strasburg, Pennsylvania, and took ten young girls hostage. In the course of the next hour, he shot all ten girls, killing five and gravely wounding the remaining five before taking his own life.

While we have come to know that each school shooting is different, the horror of the news and details shake us anew each time. And so it was at Nickel Mines, where parents, siblings, teachers, classmates, friends, and neighbors were reeling as the reality of what

60

had happened set in. So it was, too, for Charles Roberts' parents, wife, and children, whose grief was made all the more painful by the guilt they carried and the lack of even the remotest understanding of how this man—whom they thought they all knew so well—could have committed such an atrocity.

For the nation that took in this news, a second wave of shock was on its way that afternoon, as members of the Amish community came together to visit the shooter's family to extend immediate and wholehearted forgiveness. The offer was not pondered, mulled over, or questioned. This was forgiveness freely bestowed, without any requirement for repentance on the part of the perpetrator or his family. It was offered immediately, authentically, and spontaneously as a deep outpouring of their faith—from the very core of their religious training and beliefs. For the Amish, a primary tenet is to never carry a grudge. From the earliest age, lessons of forgiveness are at the heart of Sunday school and religious training. Young children are regularly taught to say, "I'm sorry" and "I forgive you."

An Amish neighbor came to Roberts's parents' home to offer forgiveness on behalf of the community. A large group went to visit Charles's widow, Marie, and her children, offering food, embraces, acceptance, and friendship, saying, "Forgiveness is a choice. We choose to forgive." Several days later, the community came out in full force to attend Roberts's funeral (which they had offered to help pay for) and to help shield the family from unrelenting media attention. Roberts's mother, Terri, later said of their neighbors' support that day, "Our son's funeral proved to be a testimony of the greatest love that anyone could show. In a world that speaks so loudly of rights, the Amish had every right to feel anger, bitterness, and thirst for revenge. Instead, we heard that day only words of kindness and compassion as they greeted Charlie's widow, Marie, his children, and our family."

Lord, make me an instrument of your peace;

Where there is hatred, let me sow love;

When there is injury, pardon;

Where there is doubt, faith;

Where there is despair, hope;

Where there is darkness, light;

And where there is sadness, joy;

O Divine Master,

Grant that I may not so much seek

To be consoled as to console;

To be understood as to understand;

To be loved as to love;

For it is in giving that we receive;

It is in pardoning that we are pardoned;

And it is in dying that we are born to eternal life.

SAINT FRANCIS OF ASSISI

In the ensuing years, the Roberts family built strong bonds with their Amish neighbors. Church members built a sunroom on the parents' house and regularly came to mow their lawn. Terri babysat and visited with the surviving victims. She gave teas for parents and children—a special one for grandparents, a swimming party for children. For many years, she spent Thursday evenings helping the most seriously wounded of the girls. Terri eventually wrote of her experience in her moving book, *Forgiven: The Amish School Shooting, A Mother's Love, and a Story of Remarkable Grace.* She lectured around the country and was often sought out for advice and comfort after other school shootings.

David L. Weaver-Zercher, Donald Kraybill, and Steven Nolt, coauthors of *Amish Grace: How Forgiveness Transcended Tragedy,* give a fuller picture of the centrality of what distinguishes forgiveness in this unique culture: "All religions teach forgiveness but the Amish are the only ones who do it." For the Amish, "Religion is not used to justify rage and revenge but to inspire goodness, forgiveness and grace." As a culture, they commit to "offer forgiveness and offer it quickly."

Skeptics may question the authenticity of a forgiveness that might, to some, seem programmed, perhaps even obligatory. No one at Nickel Mines engaged in lengthy soul-searching before stepping forward with forgiveness. The community moved unhesitatingly as one. It is impossible to predict whether the Amish ideal of forgiveness is within any individual's grasp or even something to which one would aspire, yet there are enormous lessons to be learned in observing the *effects* of forgiveness on one community: the deep bonds created, the long and sustaining friendships, and, most difficult of all, the healing of broken hearts.

IN FORGIVENESS, GOD RESIDES.

SRI KABIR JI

FORGIVENESS BREAKS THE SILOS OF A DISCONNECTED HUMANITY.

BONNIE WESORICK

TO SATAN IN HEAVEN

Forgive, Satan, virtue's pedants, all such

As have broken our habits, or had none,

The keepers of promises, prizewinners,

Meek as leaves in the wind's circus, evenings;

Our simple wish to be elsewhere forgive,

Shy touchers of library atlases,

Envious of bird-flight, the whale's submersion;

And us forgive who have forgotten how,

The melancholy who, lacing a shoe,

Choose not to continue, the merely bored,

Who have modeled our lives after cloud-shapes;

For which confessing, have mercy on us,

The different and the indifferent,

In inverse proportion to our merit,

For we have affirmed thee secretly, by

Candle-glint in the polish of silver,

Between courses, murmured amenities,

Seen thee in mirrors by morning, shaving,

Or head in loose curls on the next pillow,

Reduced thee to our own scope and purpose,

Satan, who, though in heaven, downward yearned,

As the butterfly, weary of flowers,

Longs for the cocoon or the looping net.

DONALD JUSTICE

"But I say unto you, Love your enemies,

bless them that curse you, do good to them that hate you,

and pray for them which despitefully use you, and persecute you."

MATTHEW 4:44

BODHISATTVA'S VOW

I am only a simple disciple, but I offer these respectful words:

When I look deeply into the real form of the universe,

Everything reveals the mysterious truth of the Tathagata.

This truth never fails: in every moment and every place, things
can't help but shine with this light.

Realizing this, our Ancestors gave reverent care to animals, birds,
and all beings.

Realizing this, we ourselves know that our daily food, clothing,
and shelter

are the warm body and beating heart of the Buddha.

How can we be ungrateful to anyone or anything?

Even though someone may be a fool, we can be compassionate.

If someone turns against us, speaking ill of us and treating us bitterly,

it's best to bow down:

This is the Buddha appearing to us,

Finding ways to free us from our own attachments—

the very ones that have made us suffer,

again and again and again.

Now on each flash of thought

a lotus flower blooms,

And on each flower: a buddha.

The light of the Tathagata

Appears before us, soaking into our feet.

May we share this mind with all beings,

so that we and the world together may grow in wisdom.

TOREI ENJI

WHAT POWER HAS LOVE BUT FORGIVENESS?

WILLIAM CARLOS WILLIAMS

FORGIVENESS
IS THE JOURNEY WE TAKE TOWARD HEALING OURSELVES AND OUR WORLD.

DESMOND TUTU

Eva Mozes Kor

SOME ACTS of cruelty, violence, and inhumanity are so extreme that they stretch the bounds of our compassion as we ponder what we are capable of forgiving. Are all acts forgivable? Is forgiveness even warranted in some cases? There are, of course, no hard and fast answers. But as we consider the limits of our own potential for forgiveness, it can test us in important ways to see just how far others have gone.

Eva Mozes Kor and her twin sister, Miriam, were born in 1934 on a farm in the village of Portz, Romania. The youngest children in a close-knit family, they spent their early years working on the farm and attending the local school. Like most identical twins, they were inseparable. As the only Jewish family in town, they learned about discrimination early, especially as the decade wore on. By 1940, the area had become occupied by the Nazis, and Eva and Miriam, together with their parents and two older siblings,

"Lord, forgiveness for so much cruelty."

POPE FRANCIS'S ENTRY IN THE
GUEST BOOK AT AUSCHWITZ

were forced to leave their home and move to the ghetto of Simleo Silvaniere in the Transylvania region of Romania.

One early spring day in 1944, the family was forcibly herded into a packed cattle car that would take them, along with thousands of other Jews, on a four-day journey to the notorious death camp of Auschwitz. Thrown onto the station platform, weak from lack of food or water, Eva watched as her father and older siblings were immediately dragged away. A Nazi officer asked her mother if she and Miriam were twins and, upon hearing that they were, pried the ten-year-old girls from their mother to sequester them in barracks restricted to twins ranging in age from one to thirteen.

It was here that they spent every day for the next nine months as subjects of the cruel physical experiments of Josef Mengele and the other 30 Auschwitz physicians. This "Angel of Death," as he came to be called, performed such experiments on 1,500 sets of twins during the war. Eva and her sister became desperately sick from the toxic injections they received and at times were not expected to live. As she later recounted, "Dying in Auschwitz was very easy. Surviving was a full-time job." But Eva's ferocious determination to live, and to keep her sister alive with her, saw them through to January 27, 1945, when Auschwitz and its seven thousand prisoners were liberated by the 60th Army of the First Ukrainian front, a division of the Soviet army. Eva told the full story of these months of horror in her memoir, *Surviving the Angel of Death: The True Story of a Mengele Twin in Auschwitz*, and in the documentary film *Forgiving Doctor Mengele*.

After their liberation, Eva and Miriam found their way back to their village in Romania—only to find that their home had been completely ransacked and was no longer livable. They were taken in by relatives for several years, and ultimately were able to emigrate to Israel in 1950. In 1968, Eva married a fellow Holocaust survivor and moved to Terre Haute, Indiana, where she lived until her death in 2019.

As the years wore on, Miriam felt an increasing need to confront what she had experienced at Auschwitz and give it a meaning that had thus far eluded her. By the early 1980s, Eva had located 122 other survivors of Mengele's twin experiments, living in ten countries on four continents. In 1984, with Miriam's help, Eva formed CANDLES, an acronym for Children of Auschwitz Nazi Deadly Lab Experiments, a support group for survivors and the lingering issues they lived with from this horrific time.

After Miriam's death in 1993, from effects of the Mengele experiments, Eva opened the CANDLES Holocaust Museum and Education Center in Terre Haute. In her determination to help both herself and her fellow survivors, Eva then entered the most controversial period of her life as she searched her soul to find the power to offer forgiveness to her tormentors. As she said, "Forgiveness is not so much for the perpetrator, but for the victim . . . I had the power to forgive. No one could give me that power and no one could take it away."

As part of her exploration of forgiveness, a colleague arranged for Eva to travel to Munich in 1993 to meet with Hans Münch, who had been a Nazi doctor in the Auschwitz camps. Having suffered nightmares since the war, Münch confessed to Eva that he had signed death certificates for nearly three thousand nameless victims. After absorbing this stranger's story, Eva was shocked to find that she had a degree of compassion for him, and she invited him to join her at Auschwitz on January 27, 1995, for the fiftieth anniversary of the camp's liberation. That day, standing in front of the gathering next to the ruined gas chambers, she had him sign an affidavit detailing "what he had said and seen and done, and to do it at the site of all those killings."

Three months later, deeply moved by the ceremony, Eva decided to send Münch a letter of forgiveness. Speaking of her decision, Eva says, "Immediately, I felt that a burden had been lifted from my shoulders, a pain I had lived with for fifty years; I was

"Everything can be taken from a man

but one thing; the last of the human freedoms—

to choose one's attitude in any given set of circumstances,

to choose one's own way."

VIKTOR E. FRANKL

no longer a victim of Auschwitz, no longer a victim of my tragic past. I was free." After sending her letter, she realized that there was still one additional step in forgiveness to contemplate—forgiving Mengele himself. Realizing that such an act would confirm her "new power even over the Angel of Death," she sat alone in her bedroom and spoke quietly to herself, saying, "In spite of all that, I forgive you."

Since declaring her forgiveness, Eva has been vilified by many Holocaust survivors and Jews around the world as a scandalous traitor. She fully acknowledges that her declaration was a simple, intensely personal act in order to achieve freedom for herself. She is not condoning or forgetting. She is not proselytizing or asking others to join her. "The question of justice is separate from the issue of forgiveness," she says. "This concept of forgiveness has little or nothing to do with the perpetrator. It has everything to do with the need of victims to be free from the pain inflicted upon them. . . . Do I deserve to be free from what they have done to me? Of course. My forgiveness is an act of self-healing."

As she continued to lecture around the world into her late eighties, she urged her listeners to see beyond her own personal story and contemplate how much forgiveness they could bring into their own lives, in far less dramatic ways. She urged educators to teach young children the power of forgiveness, of caring for one another, and of extending friendship to the ostracized—sowing the seeds for lives less marked by violence, anger, and blame. "Anger and hate are seeds that germinate war," Eva says. "Forgiveness is a seed for peace."

"If only there were evil people somewhere

insidiously committing evil deeds, and it were necessary only to

separate them from the rest of us and destroy them! But the line

dividing good and evil cuts through the heart of every human

being. And who is willing to destroy a piece of his own heart?"

ALEKSANDR SOLZHENITSYN

FORGIVENESS

Where you are the temperature plummets
At night, and you sleep in the open
And just gravity holds you. The dry riverbeds
Are both penance and reward. I know you've walked
miles now, and you've scattered the last of me

into the pines and box canyons and dust,
into whatever the wind carries and loses,
into a country whose language I don't speak.
So the thoughts you send me now become gestures,
hands pocketed and unpocketed before you move on,

and in my dreams you take on a terrible solidity.
You wear that guilt-laced anger I've seen men mask—
like an old lover of mine who whispered through his embrace,
Omit me from what you have written. You I omit
the way an artist draws with an eraser,

absence taking tangible shape from the darkness.
Whether each of us has exiled within ourselves a memory
we can trust to find its way, or one crippled with lies,
we're learning that the fugitive past can cover
its tracks, but not erase them; that out of love

and grief, it takes the shape of our shadows,
crouches by trash cans in the mind's back alleys,
surviving on what we refuse. Look above it, instead,
and say that in time the unreconciled settles into place
like a renegade star in some guiding constellation,

and that our altered courses remain the correct ones.
That's what I tell myself in these northern woods.
I call your abandonment grace and believe in it
even more than you. That I might finally move
through this meanwhile and find a place to live.

DEBRA ALLBERY

"When you release the wrongdoer

from the wrong, you cut a malignant tumor out

of your inner life. You set a prisoner free,

but you discover that the real prisoner was yourself."

LEWIS B. SMEDES

"Forgiveness has nothing to do with absolving a criminal of his crime. It has everything to do with relieving oneself of the burden of being a victim—letting go of the pain and transforming oneself from victim to survivor."

C. R. STRAHAN

THE REST

The rest of us watch from beyond the fence
as the woman moves with her jagged stride
into her pain as if into a slow race.
We see her body in motion
but hear no sounds, or we hear
sounds but no language; or we know
it is not a language we know
yet. We can see her clearly
but for her it is running in black smoke.
The cluster of cells in her swelling
like porridge boiling, and bursting,

like grapes, we think. Or we think of
explosions in mud; but we know nothing.
All around us the trees
and the grasses light up with forgiveness,
so green and at this time
of the year healthy.
We would like to call something
out to her. Some form of cheering.
There is pain but no arrival at anything.

MARGARET ATWOOD

FREE PEOPLE ARE NOT CHAINED TO RESENTMENT.

NADIA BOLZ-WEBER

"Forgiveness is not a lack of discrimination

whereby we let all the criminals out of prison; it is an attitude

that permits us to relate to the pain that led to their errors

and recognize their need for love."

JOAN BORYSENKO

Gill Hicks

SOMETIMES a life of forgiveness can unfold from the simple act of choosing not to blame, harbor anger, or hold grudges. Forgiveness is always a choice—often one that comes out of quite desperate situations.

In July 2005, Gill Hicks, a native Australian living in London, seemed to have everything. She was young and successful executive at London's Design Council, and recently engaged to a man she adored. She had come to London only a few years earlier, and had been able to create a life far beyond her childhood dreams.

A self-confessed workaholic, Gill was always at her desk by 7:30 in the morning. But on July 7, she lingered at home for an extra hour. Then, with rush hour in full swing, she pushed her way into the crowded car at her usual Russell Square Tube station. Nothing seemed out of the ordinary. The morning had all the hallmarks of every workday morning of her London life. But seconds after the doors closed, in the time it took to

IF YOU WANT TO SEE THE

HEROIC,

LOOK AT THOSE

WHO CAN LOVE

IN RETURN FOR HATRED.

IF YOU WANT TO SEE THE

BRAVE,

LOOK AT THOSE WHO CAN

FORGIVE. BHAGAVAD GITA

blink her eyes, Gill was lying on the car's floor in total darkness, surrounded by smoke and the screams of her fellow passengers.

Gill's late departure that day had put her in a car with Germaine Lindsay, a 19 year old Al-Qaeda–inspired suicide bomber who, at 8:59, detonated the device he had strapped to his body. At the same time, his three fellow bombers struck throughout London, killing 52 and wounding hundreds of others.

Gill's memory of lying in the chaotic aftermath of the explosion remains vivid. Realizing that her legs were badly damaged, she had the presence of mind to make two tourniquets from her scarves. She intentionally slowed her breathing and fought to stay awake and call out for help. It was an hour before emergency workers reached her and transported her to St. Thomas' Hospital. Now unconscious, unrecognizable, and near death, she was admitted bearing the hospital bracelet of "one unknown, estimated female."

Surviving surgeries to amputate both legs and spending many days in a coma, Gill hung on to life by a thread, her fiancé, Joe, holding her hand throughout. What followed were months in the hospital as she slowly regained strength and embarked on a long, rigorous physical therapy that would eventually have her walking out of the hospital with her new prosthetic legs a few months later—and, in December, up the aisle of St. Etheldreda's Church, where she and Joe were married.

Gill's time in the hospital also provided a prolonged reflective space in which to ponder what had happened to her, and how to rebuild the precious life that she could now reclaim. "My decision was to be a survivor and not a victim of the bombings," she said. "I could have let hatred for this act and for the person who committed it consume me. I vowed I would never take anything—all that I have—for granted again. I would never forget how precious every single day is."

"Instead of thinking, 'I will not forgive

that person because . . .' shift it to 'I choose to hold on

to resentment and all that pain because . . .'

How does holding on to that pain really help your life?

What benefit is there for you to keep it alive?

Once you make that shift inside, you will always find reason

to forgive, and will never find reason not to. The key benefit

of forgiving is the freedom to love and trust again."

DOE ZANTAMATA

We often hear people who have experienced terrifying events and grave illnesses share how lucky they are, how their lives have been granted extraordinary meaning in their new reality. Says Gill, "In many ways, I'm very fortunate. I have found a clarity that I never expected or knew could exist. Being high on life gave me and continues to give me the ability to find the positives in nearly all situations. I feel liberated!"

When Gill was able to return to her old job, she soon realized that the inner shift her experience had prompted required a wholly different focus of her professional energy. She felt on fire with the desire to make a difference in the world, "with the belief that the cycle of violence has to end with each of us. We all have within us the power to say 'No, I will not retaliate,' or 'I will not seek revenge.'"

Now an international motivational speaker and writer, Gill founded M.A.D. (Making a Difference) for Peace, and sees her role as that of advocate and messenger for peace. At M.A.D., she uses her experience to build empathic communities in which, as she says, "We can step into the other's shoes." She has tried to bring this empathy even to the bomber, realizing that his act was not personal to her. She had not been the enemy.

Gill continues to be guided by the words on her hospital bracelet: *one unknown*. That day on the train, she was a human being whose race, gender, name, and profession didn't matter. She was a human being worth saving and, as the result of the violent act of a stranger, she is now a human being dedicated to bringing more peace into the world in order to save countless other "unknowns."

"To forgive is to put oneself in a larger gravitational field of experience than the one that first seemed to hurt us."

DAVID WHYTE

AS LONG AS YOU DON'T
FORGIVE,
WHO AND WHATEVER IT IS
WILL OCCUPY
RENT-FREE SPACE
IN YOUR MIND.

ISABELLE HOLLAND

"Guilt, regret, resentment, sadness

and all forms of nonforgiveness are caused

by too much past and not enough presence."

ECKHART TOLLE

FORGIVENESS
IS NOT AN
OCCASIONAL ACT,
IT IS A CONSTANT
ATTITUDE.

MARTIN LUTHER KING JR.

MY SKULL

Finally, dear skull, your appearance
delights me. For so long
I've known you were coming.
I saw it in my father and uncles,
I caught glimpses so soon
after puberty, that while a long
and thick mop of hair hung
below my shoulders there was
what seemed a constant breeze,
a headwind pushing the hair away
from my forehead, back, always back.
And with the sun blazing
through the thinning strands, you,
dear skull, blazed back.
It's gotten so that I wouldn't
recognize myself with too much hair,

nor do I think I would like who I saw:
that man, with a mouth of big teeth,
the face of a giant ant, and those eyes. . .
those eyes I've seen in photographs
when I was looking elsewhere—
the eyes of a blackbird, a scavenger
groveling and pecking, flying away
at the slightest noise. Silent cranium,
passing through it all: the odd jobs,
the inclement weather, the few hands
that have tousled my hair and rubbed
you, dear skull, the monk in me,
patiently making your way
to the clear sky
to bow.

SEIDO RAY RONCI

> "WE CANNOT LOVE UNLESS WE HAVE ACCEPTED
> FORGIVENESS, AND THE DEEPER OUR EXPERIENCE
> OF FORGIVENESS IS, THE GREATER IS OUR LOVE."
>
> PAUL TILLICH

Immaculée Ilibagiza

SOMETIMES CALLED "the jewel of Africa," the small country of Rwanda, the size of the state of Maryland, is a land of lush valleys, terraced hillsides, volcanic mountains, and crystal-clear lakes. As Immaculée Ilibagiza says, "I was born in Paradise!" Her close and loving family and community of caring neighbors were part of that paradise. Her parents were hardworking teachers and farmers whom she shared with three brothers. With his own two hands, her father built their family home—in the village of Mataba, overlooking beautiful Lake Kivu in the western province of Kibuye—as a present for her mother. Immaculée's early memories are dominated by idyllic days on the land, childhood play with siblings and friends, and close ties to loving neighbors.

But even amidst this happiness, there were rumblings of what was to come. Daily life was mostly peaceful, but there had been long-standing friction between the country's

ANGER MAKES YOU SMALLER,
WHILE FORGIVENESS
FORCES YOU TO GROW
BEYOND WHAT YOU WERE.

CHERIE CARTER SCOTT

Tutsi and Hutu tribes. Immaculée remembers her shock when one day her Hutu elementary school teacher asked all the Hutu students in the class to stand. Not even knowing to which tribe her family belonged, Immaculée was derided by the teacher for her ignorance of her "inferior" Tutsi status. Her parents later explained the racial division, but it had very little impact on the next few years of her life in school and then as a privileged student in the place she won through her hard work at the Lycée.

Brilliant, diligent, and determined to earn the best possible education for herself despite the family's modest circumstances, Immaculée was awarded a full scholarship to the University of Rwanda, where she began studying electrical and mechanical engineering in 1991. University life opened her eyes to both a world of new knowledge and the wider world of the increasingly explosive racial struggles unfolding in Rwanda. At first, it was perplexing. But, as the conflict increased during her time at university, it grew increasingly frightening. In her third year, the danger became both severe and widespread as Hutus began to attack their Tutsi neighbors.

During the Easter Break of 1994, as the violence increased, Immaculée's father pleaded with her to come home. That April, Rwandan president Juvenal Habyarimana—a Hutu—died when his plane was shot down above Kigali airport. The event ignited full-out war as Hutus now began to go house to house, viciously slaughtering their Tutsi neighbors. Immaculée was no longer safe at university or at home. The unbridled Hutu anger cut down any Tutsi in its path.

With the killing now moving into their village, Immaculée's father could find no solution that would allow the family to stay together. With mortal danger on their doorstep, he walked Immaculée to the house of a Hutu pastor who had always been a trusted friend, and she begged him to hide her. Realizing the danger this move would place him in, Pastor Murinzi reluctantly acquiesced and hid Immaculée in a 3-by-5-foot bathroom

"Forgiveness is the economy of the heart.

Forgiveness saves the expense of anger,

the cost of hatred, the waste of spirits."

HANNAH MORE

off his bedroom, covering the door with a large wardrobe. Soon she was joined by seven other Tutsi women, ranging in age from seven to 55. It was in this tiny space, unable to move or speak, that these women were to spend the next 91 days.

During their time in hiding, they were constantly assaulted by the cries of machete-wielding Hutu soldiers, usually hundreds at a time. They broke into the pastor's house searching for her, or stood outside her window, glorifying their mission of torture and death and chanting her name. She heard constant screaming from those being tortured and killed, as well as the killers' gleeful boasts.

To survive this time in hiding, Immaculée drew from almost superhuman determination and faith, as well as her strong religious upbringing. Gripping her father's rosary, she spent up to 20 hours a day in prayer. She surprised herself by finding that her prayers were not only for herself and her family but, most remarkably, for the killers as well. "I took a crucial step of forgiving the killers," she reflects. "My anger was draining from me. For the first time, I pitied the killers. That night I prayed with a clear conscience and a clean heart. For the first time since I entered the bathroom, I slept in peace."

Immaculée's abiity to forgive was what kept her from giving up. She came close more than once, but was always able to bring herself back from the brink of total despair. When death seemed a breath away, she repeated over and over: "Forgive them!"

After three months, a small contingent of French soldiers arrived in Rwanda to provide safe havens for the Tutsi survivors and to help bring about the first steps toward peace. Now an emaciated 65 pounds (she went into hiding weighing 115), Immaculée and her seven fellow survivors made their way to a series of French refugee camps. Each journey and camp brought near-death experiences along the road. But luck, faith, and the help of strangers carried them to each new place. At one camp, a soldier who was so enraged by what Immaculée had endured offered to kill those responsible for her family's murder if only she would name them. "The captain's anger made me think that the cycle of hatred and mistrust in Rwanda would not easily be broken," she recalls. "There would certainly be even more bitterness after the killing stopped, bitterness that could easily erupt into more violence. . . I could see that helping others to forgive would be a big part of my life's work."

Once it was relatively safe, a circuitous path led Immaculée to Rwanda's capital, to many arms outstretched in help and ultimately to a career with the United Nations, first in Kigali and, after a few years, in New York. Along this path of reentering life, she was offered the opportunity to return to her village and meet with her parents' killer—a meeting that was to test her now well-honed ability to forgive. "I wept at the sight of his suffering. Felicien (the killer) had let the devil enter his heart, and the evil had ruined his life like a cancer in his soul. He was now the victim of his victims, destined to live in torment and regret. I was overwhelmed with pity for the way Felicien was sobbing. I could feel his shame. He looked up at me for only a moment, but our eyes met. I reached out, touched his hands lightly, and quietly said what I'd come to say: 'I forgive you.'"

This climactic moment in her life was both an end and a beginning. Resettled in the United States, Immaculée married, raised a family, and is now an inspirational writer and speaker on forgiveness, as well as head of her own foundation supporting Rwandan student sponsorships and a new seminary in Rwanda. "Forgiveness," she says, "is all I have to offer."

FORGIVENESS

Forgiveness is the fragrance, rare and sweet,

That flowers yield when trampled on by feet

That reckless tread the tender, teeming earth;

For blossoms crushed and bleeding yet give birth

To pardon's perfume; from the stern decrees

Of unforgiveness. Nature ever flees.

ELLA A. GILES

"Forgiving is a selfish act to free yourself from being controlled by your past."

EVA EIGER

TRUE FORGIVENESS

IS NOT AN ACTION AFTER THE FACT,

IT IS AN ATTITUDE

WITH WHICH YOU ENTER

EACH MOMENT.

DAVID RIDGE

FORGIVENESS . . . A VERY GOOD UNDERSTANDING OF FORGIVENESS

One of my teachers had each of us bring a clear plastic bag and
a sack of potatoes.

For every person we'd refuse to forgive in our life, we were told
to choose a potato,

write on it the name and date, and put it in the plastic bag.

Some of our bags, as you can imagine, were quite heavy.

We were then told to carry this bag with us everywhere for one week,

putting it beside our bed at night, on the car seat when driving,
next to our desk at work.

The hassle of lugging this around with us

made it clear what a weight we were carrying spiritually,

and how we had to pay attention to it all the time to not forget,

and keep leaving it in embarrassing places.

Naturally, the condition of the potatoes deteriorated to a nasty slime.

This was a great metaphor for the price we pay

For keeping our pain and heavy negativity!

Too often we think of forgiveness as a gift to the other person,

And while that's true . . . it clearly is also a gift for ourselves!

So the next time you decide you can't forgive someone, ask yourself . . .

Isn't *my* bag heavy enough?

Tafadzwa Mhondiwa Mugari

THE INEFFABLE JOY OF FORGIVING AND BEING FORGIVEN FORMS AN ECSTASY THAT MIGHT WELL AROUSE THE ENVY OF THE GODS.

ELBERT HUBBARD

"And when a man injures and oppresses you and deals unjustly with you, you should deal kindly with him and forgive him. Thus you will strike at the root of hatred and enmity and he who is your enemy will become your friend."

THE QURAN

A SETTLEMENT

Look, it's spring. And last year's loose dust has turned into this soft willingness. The wind-flowers have come up trembling, slowly the brackens are up-lifting their curvaceous and pale bodies. The thrushes have come home, none less than filled with mystery, sorrow, happiness, music ambition.

And I am walking out into all of this with nowhere to go and no task undertaken but to turn the pages of this beautiful world over and over, in the world of my mind.

* * *

Therefore, dark past,
I'm about to do it.
I'm about to forgive you

for everything.

MARY OLIVER

> "WHEN WE FORGIVE, WE COME AS CLOSE AS ANY HUMAN BEING CAN TO THE ESSENTIALLY DIVINE ACT OF CREATION. FOR WE CREATE A NEW BEGINNING OUT OF PAST PAIN . . ."
>
> LEWIS B. SMEDES

The Emanuel Nine

Cynthia Marie Graham Hurd, Susie Jackson, Ethel Lee Lance, The Reverend DePayne Middleton-Doctor, The Reverend Clementa Pinckney, Tywanza Sanders, The Reverend Daniel Simmons, The Reverend Sharonda Coleman-Singleton, Myra Thompson

ON THE evening of June 17, 2015, the weekly Bible Study class at the historic Emanuel A.M.E. Church in Charleston, South Carolina, was just getting under way when a young white man appeared at the African-American gathering and asked to join the class. The Reverend Clementa Pinckney invited him to come in and sit beside him. As the class came to a close after an hour, the group bowed their heads and closed their

GOOD-NATURE & GOOD SENSE

MUST EVER JOIN;

TO ERR IS HUMAN;

TO FORGIVE, DIVINE.

ALEXANDER POPE

eyes in prayer. In that moment, the young visitor pulled out his many loaded weapons and opened fire on the group, killing nine and wounding five.

In the days and now years since that soul-crushing event, we have risked growing numb, as the number of similar shootings, claiming countless innocent lives, has escalated beyond anything we could have then imagined.

In the hours that followed, as relatives and friends of the dead came to identify them, our hearts bled for their collective grief. But we were unprepared for the words of some of the relatives to the shooter as he was arraigned for these murders the next day.

Nadine Collier, daughter of 70-year-old victim Ethel Lance, said: "I will never talk to her ever again, I will never be able to hold her again, but I forgive you, and have mercy on your soul. You hurt me. You hurt a lot of people . . . but God forgives you and I forgive you."

Another relative: "I forgive you for your actions. Forgiveness is the heartbeat that pulls us to another level."

And another: "Hate won't win."

Known as "Mother Emanuel," this remarkable church community traces its roots to 1816, when free and enslaved blacks who had withdrawn from Charleston's Methodist church over discriminatory worship practices affiliated with the recently formed African Methodist Episcopal denomination, becoming the first A.M.E. congregation in the South. This white supremacist shooter not only shot down nine beloved and admired members of the church, but also struck at the very heart of the larger community of African-American houses of worship. While he shot viciously at random, his selection of his target was hardly random. Since the day of the shooting, the murderer has never expressed regret or remorse, instead claiming that he is proud of what he did.

Not everyone forgave in the immediate aftermath of the killings. But those who did

"When you forgive me for harming you,

you decide not to retaliate, to seek no revenge. You don't have

to like me. You simply unburden yourself of the weight of

resentment and cut the cycle of retribution that would otherwise

keep us ensnared in an ugly samsaric wrestling match. This is

a gift you can give us both, totally on your own, without my

having to know or understand what you've done."

THANISSARO BHIKKHU

ascribed their ability to do so to their Christian faith, which they felt demanded their forgiveness, even in the midst of nearly unimaginable horror.

With time to grieve between the killing and the sentencing after the young man's trial, many relatives found their way to standing in the light of forgiveness. After Dylann Roof was sentenced to death following a three-hour jury deliberation, thirty relatives stepped forward to address him in the courtroom. Sitting motionless with his eyes firmly fixed on the table ahead of him, Roof did not look up at any of the speakers. Many tried to get his attention, asking him to look them in the eye. His demeanor and lack of regret would be enough to harden any soul. But the community chose another path.

Felicia Sanders, a survivor of the shooting, lost her son Tywanza and her aunt Susie Jackson. A member of the sixth generation of her family to worship at the church, Felicia addressed Roof after he was sentenced, saying, "Yes, I forgive you. That was the easiest thing I had to do. May God have mercy on your soul."

Melvin Graham, brother of victim Cynthia Graham Hurd, summed up what had happened in the church community, the city of Charleston, and across the country in the wake of this horror: "Instead of starting a race war, you started a love war."

One of the greatest gifts that the forgiving spirit at Mother Emanuel gave us all was the sense that forgiveness can be contagious. We were all entitled to remain in shock and rage, to poison our world with continuing anger. But witnessing the love and compassion of those for whom the grief was greatest turned many of our hearts and minds around. Instead of looting, there was praying. Many relatives of the victims now travel around the country speaking about the power of forgiveness.

In one of his recent speeches, the Reverend Anthony Thompson, who lost his wife that day, described how that power has changed his life:

I could feel everything—bitterness, anger, hate, the way I felt about my wife and how I was missing her—literally leaving my body. I had a peace like no other. I felt light as a feather. Peace that passeth all understanding is real. I preached that sermon I don't know how many times, and I told people how I thought it was, and never knew until that moment. I felt it, and I still feel it, right now, today. My new mission is to spread the gospel of forgiveness. And doing that, I've seen a lot of people's lives change.

Three years later, Charleston finalized plans for two beautiful memorial spaces—a stone courtyard and a grassy garden—designed by the architect of the September 11 memorial in New York City. The memorial is, of course, meant for the victims and survivors. But it is also a commemoration of the strong and resilient spirit of forgiveness that has proven to be so contagious. As one church member put it: "Forgiveness is now healing Charleston where people are reaching across the barriers, bringing down walls. That is what forgiveness is doing for us—healing our city."

Forgiveness can be a choice, if we can find the power to open our hearts and minds to it.

NEVER FORGET

THE THREE POWERFUL RESOURCES

YOU ALWAYS HAVE AVAILABLE TO YOU:

LOVE · PRAYER ·

AND FORGIVENESS.

H. JACKSON BROWN JR.

THE CALL

I have heard it all my life.
A voice calling a name I recognized as my own.

Sometimes it comes as a soft-bellied whisper.
Sometimes it holds an edge of urgency.

But always it says: Wake up, my love. You are walking asleep.
There's no safety in that!

Remember what you are, and let this knowing
take you home to the Beloved with every breath.

Hold tenderly who you are and let a deeper knowing
color the shape of your humanness.

There is nowhere to go. What you are looking for is right here.
Open the fist clenched in wanting and see what you already
hold in your hand.

There is no waiting for something to happen.
no point in the future to get to.
All you have ever longed for is here in this moment, right now.

You are wearing yourself out with all this searching.
Come home and rest.

How much longer can you live like this?
Your hungry spirit is gaunt, your heart stumbles. All this trying,
Give it up!

Let yourself be one of the God-mad,
faithful only to the Beauty you are.

Let the Lover pull you to your feet and hold you close,
dancing even when fear urges you to sit this one out.

Remember, there is one word you are here to say with your whole being.
When it finds you, give your life to it. Don't be tight-lipped and stingy.

Spend yourself completely on the saying,
Be one word in this great love poem we are writing together.

ORIAH MOUNTAIN DREAMER

"Mercy is radical kindness.

Mercy means offering or being offered aid in desperate straits.

Mercy is not deserved. It involves absolving the unabsolvable,

forgiving the unforgivable. Mercy brings us to the miracle

of apology, given and accepted, to unashamed humility

when we have erred or forgotten."

ANNE LAMOTT

TRUE FORGIVENESS

DOES NOT DENY THE SUFFERING

OF THE PAST BUT HAS TREMENDOUS

DIGNITY & COURAGE &

POWER OF LOVE IN IT

THAT SAYS

WE WILL, AND CAN,

START AGAIN.

JACK KORNFIELD

ONE FORGIVES
TO THE DEGREE THAT
ONE LOVES.

FRANCOIS DE LA ROCHEFOUCAULD

"The act of apology and forgiveness is like a sacrament of human community. It is how we remember who we really are to each other."

ROSEMARIE FREENEY HARDING

FORGIVENESS
IS THE FINAL FORM
OF LOVE.

REINHOLD NIEBUHR

Will Morales

WHILE FOR SOME, self-forgiveness is the toughest challenge, for others, like Will Morales, self-forgiveness is the first step in creating a new life—one in which forgiveness is the driving force.

Will says that he was "raised in hate," in a world where conflict was always met with aggression. From a young age, he witnessed his heroin-addicted father violently beat his mother, then take her money to buy drugs. When he was eight years old, he witnessed his uncle's violent death. Will learned early to hide his hurt by hurting others, to stay quiet, and not to show any emotion.

To escape her husband, Will's mother secretly took him and his younger brother from Brooklyn to Boston to start a new life far from anyone who knew them. Will struggled in a new school as he and his family moved from one rented bedroom to another. At age 12, in response to poverty and a sense of having no other way out, Will turned to

IF I CANNOT FORGIVE MYSELF

If I cannot forgive myself
For all the blunders
That I have made
Over the years,
Then how can I proceed?
How can I ever
Dream perfection-dreams?
Move, I must, forward.
Fly, I must, upward.
Dive, I must, inward,
To be once more
What I truly am
And shall forever remain.

SRI CHINMOY

what felt like his only option—joining a gang and selling crack on the streets. At 16, he was arrested and sent to prison for stabbing and shooting two men.

Life in prison proved even more violent than it had been on the streets. It felt, to Will, like a rite of passage, marked by rituals of hatred. During his time behind bars, he never witnessed even a single act of compassion or forgiveness—until the night that he received an emergency phone call informing him that his brother had been killed by the police.

Because violence was all he had known, Will's immediate response was to vow to find and kill the officers responsible for his brother's death as soon as he was free. It was the only way he knew to react to pain and loss. But then came an unexpected turning point. As he was reeling from the news, a prison official gave Will his first experience of care, understanding, and help from a stranger. Seeing his pain, the official reached out to gently touch his elbow, saying simply, "I am deeply sorry for your loss."

At a moment in which Will had expected silence and the order to return to his cell, this stranger offered to sit with him and allow him to process the shock of the tragic news. What made this single, unexpected gesture even more powerful was the fact that it came from what Will later called "a part of the system that wanted to drop me into the wastebasket."

In that moment of being seen and understood, Will was able to hit the *pause* button. And what he realized was that his anger was really directed at himself. He blamed himself for his brother's death. For the first time, he felt humility in the face of his struggles, and decided to do something with his life. Reflecting on that pivotal night, Will says it was the beginning of his process of rethinking "how I engage and connect with people . . . I began to look at people knowing that they have their own struggles and stories."

A second surprise awaited in the following days, when the prison warden breached

"Forgiving does not erase the bitter past.

A healed memory is not a deleted memory.

Instead, forgiving what we cannot forget

creates a new way to remember.

We change the memory of our past

into a hope for our future."

LEWIS B. SMEDES

protocol to allow Will's family and pastor to perform a memorial service for his brother in the prison, open to any inmates who wanted to attend. He soon learned that his fellow prisoners had contributed to a memorial fund from their commissary accounts. In the midst of a tragic loss, Will clearly saw that "there are people out there who care, and I need to demonstrate care in my own life."

Will knew that, in order to chart a new course, he would need to understand how he had arrived at this moment. He took stock of where he was, and how and why he had gotten there, and seized the one positive thing that his remaining years in prison could give him—the time to examine his past, to stop indulging in excuses, to study and prepare for the life he wanted.

Leaving prison with high hopes, he returned to a community where he no longer fit in, a community that did not want him. Homeless and with few prospects, he chose to understand rather than blame. As an early step in forging his new life, he contacted the two people he had injured to ask for their forgiveness. Looking back on both incidents, he realized that he had known each time that he had a choice to turn away and not act on his anger. Instead, he gave in to the feeling of hate "moving through my body," as indeed it always had. Now he had the opportunity to make amends to his mother, his brother, his victims, his community, and himself.

At so many of the important junctures in Will's life, there had been a clear choice between hatred and violence or understanding and forgiveness. Embracing the latter, he visited with the two police officers who had killed his brother—a meeting that led to their ultimately becoming friends. He was able to see that "they were just doing their job. You do what you have to do. I think they struggled afterward." With the desire to reset his compass in the direction of forgiveness, Will searched for new role models, and the help he needed began to flow his way in the form of people who believed in him, supported him in planning a new future, and provided the connections and counsel he needed in order to become for other young people "the person who wasn't there for me . . . I wanted to take what I had learned and change lives."

Will's early work with young people led to the formation of the Boston Youth and Police Partnership, the first outreach program in the city's history created by teenagers. He went on to earn a bachelor's degree in criminal justice and then an MBA, and directed youth services in leadership positions first at Wheelock College and then for the YMCA of Greater Boston. In 2016, Will was appointed Commissioner of Boston Centers for Youth and Families, and became a key member of the Mayor's Health and Services Cabinet. In overseeing a network of 36 facilities and 30 community centers throughout Boston, serving more than 90,000 people annually, he is committed to "serving as a tangible example of forgiveness, and that hate never works."

In many ways, Will Morales seems the very embodiment of the power of compassion and forgiveness to change lives—sometimes in the space of a single moment.

FORGIVENESS IS
GIVING UP ALL HOPE
OF A BETTER PAST.

VARIOUSLY ATTRIBUTED

FORGIVENESS

Each moment things forgive you. All your hours
Are crowded with rich penitence unknown
Even to you. Shot birds and trampled flowers,
And worms that you have murdered with a stone
In idle sport—yea, and the well whose deep,
Translucent, green and solitary sleep
You stirred into harsh wrinkles with a stick.
Red mud that you have bound into a brick,
Old wood that you have wrought into bark,
Flame in the street-lamp held to light the dark,
And fierce red rubies chiselled for a ring . . .
You are forgiven each hour by everything!

HARINDRANATH CHATTOPADHYAYA

"Forgiveness is the answer to the child's dream

of a miracle by which what is broken is made whole again,

what is soiled is made clean again."

DAG HAMMARSKJÖLD

"Forgiveness is giving up the right to retaliate.

Forgiveness is the willingness to have something happen the way

it happened. It's not true that you can't forgive something;

it's a matter of the will, and you always have the choice.

Forgiveness is never dependent on what the other person does

or does not do; it is always under our control. Forgiveness is

giving up the insistence on being understood."

PIXIE KOESTLINE HAMMOND

FORGIVING MY FATHER

it is Friday, we have come
to the paying of the bills.
all week you have stood in my dreams
like a ghost, asking for more time
but today is payday, payday old man;
my mother's hand opens in her early grave
and i hold it out like a good daughter.

there is no more time for you. there will
never be time enough daddy daddy old lecher
old liar. i wish you were rich so i could take it all
and give the lady what she was due
but you were the only son of a needy father,
the father of a needy son;
you gave her all you had
which was nothing. you have already given her
all you had.

you are the pocket that was going to open
and come up empty any friday.

you were each other's bad bargain, not mine.
daddy old pauper old prisoner, old dead man
what am I doing here collecting?
you lie side by side in debtors' boxes
and no accounting will open them up.

LUCILLE CLIFTON

RAGING

AGAINST ANOTHER PERSON

IS LIKE **DRINKING POISON**

AND EXPECTING

THE **OTHER PERSON** TO DIE.

VARIOUSLY ATTRIBUTED

"Forgive, forget. Bear with the faults of others as you would have them bear with yours. Be patient and understanding. Life is too short to be vengeful or malicious."

PHILLIPS BROOKS

FOR LOST FRIENDS

As twilight makes a rainbow robe
From the concealed colors of day
In order for time to stay alive
Within the dark weight of night,
May we lose no one we love
From the shelter of our hearts.

When we love another heart
And allow it to love us,
We journey deep below time
Into that eternal weave
Where nothing unravels.

May we have the grace to see
Despite the hurt of rupture,
The searing of anger,
And the empty disappointment,
That whoever we have loved,
Such love can never quench.

Though a door may have closed,
Closed between us,
May we be able to view
Our lost friends with eyes
Wise with calming grace;
Forgive them the damage
We were left to inherit;

Free ourselves from the chains
Of forlorn resentment;
Bring warmth again to
Where the heart has frozen
In order that beyond the walls
Of our cherished hurt
And chosen distance
We may be able to
Celebrate the gifts they
brought,
Learn and grow from the pain,
And prosper into difference,
Wishing them the peace
Where spirit can summon
Beauty from wounded space.

JOHN O'DONOHUE

"YOU HAVE TO SAY 'I AM FORGIVEN' AGAIN
AND AGAIN UNTIL IT BECOMES THE STORY
YOU BELIEVE ABOUT YOURSELF."

CHERYL STRAYED

Sue Klebold

SUE KLEBOLD'S LIFE has been written about and analyzed from nearly every conceivable angle. But little attention has been paid to what I consider her greatest challenge and her greatest teaching for us all—how we can cultivate self-compassion, even self-forgiveness, in the face of paralyzing guilt and shame.

April 20, 1999 was an especially beautiful early-spring day in the Rocky Mountain foothills. Sue's son, Dylan—who had just attended his senior prom and was anticipating his graduation from high school in a few weeks and a new life at college in the fall—headed out the door early for school, calling out a quick "Bye" to Sue and her husband, Tom, from the door. Sue had no idea that within a few hours a catastrophe of earth-shattering proportions would both transform and define her life.

Dylan Klebold and his classmate Eric Harris were about to become the infamous

"Because forgiveness is like this:

a room can be dank because you have closed the windows,

you've closed the curtains. But the sun is shining outside,

and the air is fresh outside. In order to get that fresh air,

you have to get up and open the window and draw

the curtains apart."

DESMOND TUTU

Columbine killers. Using an arsenal of bombs, guns, and other weapons, they carried out a massacre that killed twelve students and one teacher, wounded another 20, and forever changed the lives of countless families, communities, and the nation. In a sense, we all lost part of our innocence that day. Sue lost hers forever.

Many of us who remember the news accounts that day can still feel the shock and disbelief. But it stretches all bounds of our imagination to try to put ourselves in the shoes of a mother hearing that there had been a shooting at her son's school, living through a day of not knowing if he were safe, and then coming face to face with the fact that it was her beloved son who had perpetrated the murders and then ended his own life.

To read Sue's account of that day in her powerful book, *A Mother's Reckoning: Living in the Aftermath of Tragedy*, is to step into her shoes and experience the unimaginable. With a clear-eyed candor, won through excruciating years of reflection, soul searching, and professional help, Sue examines every detail of Dylan's early life, especially the year before his death, scanning each moment in her painful search for what could have led this loving and beloved young man to commit this horror. She read his diaries and went through everything he left behind. She scoured home videos of his childhood and footage of the shootings. She wholly committed herself to the search for understanding.

At the very core of this search are always her recurring questions: How could she have not known? What clues did she miss? What could she have done to change the course of events? How could she have let down this young man whom she loved so much? "Sixteen years have passed since that terrible day, and I have dedicated them to understanding what is still incomprehensible to me—how a promising boy's life could have escalated into such a disaster, and on my watch," she writes. "A day does not pass that I do not feel a sense of overwhelming guilt—both for the myriad ways I failed Dylan and for the destruction he left in his wake."

HE THAT CANNOT
FORGIVE OTHERS
BREAKS THE BRIDGE OVER WHICH
HE MUST PASS HIMSELF;
FOR EVERY MAN HAS NEED
TO BE FORGIVEN.

THOMAS FULLER

All childhoods, and especially the adolescent years, have their bumpy moments that leave parents scratching their heads. Dylan's seemed no different. The more she searched for clues, the more Sue became convinced that "anyone could be here." Many families never know the extent of a young person's pain and destructiveness until it is too late. For Sue and Tom, "Our first inkling that something was seriously wrong slammed into our lives in one catastrophic, irreversible moment."

Many years later, a friend asked Sue if she could ever forgive Dylan. Her response goes to the heart of her continuing struggle. "Forgive Dylan? My work is to forgive *myself*. . . . I was the one who let *him* down, not the other way around." When asked what she would say to Dylan now, she responds, "I would ask him to forgive me, for being his mother and never knowing what was going on inside his head, for not being able to help him, for not being the person that he could confide in."

Over the long years of attempting to create a life of meaning and purpose for herself, Sue has become a passionate advocate for suicide prevention and mental-health counseling, speaking throughout the country to professionals, communities, and families. The publication of her book, the proceeds of which she donates to suicide prevention organizations, and the press interviews that followed served to bring these difficult subjects to audiences in new and powerful ways.

I have known Sue and her family since our early school years together in Columbus, Ohio. Her sister, Diane, was my closest friend. I adored her beautiful mother, Charlotte. I probably spent more time in their home than in any other than my own in those years. This was a loving, close-knit circle of wonderful people. To read Sue's book is to see that loving background alive in her own family. Family was everything to them. Against this backdrop, the horror she has lived through is particularly chilling.

I asked Sue about self-forgiveness and why it is so impossible for us to bestow it on ourselves. If we are up to the task, how can extending compassion to ourselves change our own lives and the lives of those around us? Is it possible to cultivate good from this pain?

"I've come to accept that I will never completely forgive myself," she told me. "It was my job to love and protect my son. I failed to protect him, but I still love him. What I share with people when they lose others is that it's okay not to forgive yourself. It's normal. Why beat yourself up for feeling what you feel? You have plenty of other reasons to beat yourself up. Embrace that feeling and use it to honor the person you love. I can't count the wonderful people I've met whose commitment to change things grew from a personal loss or failure. For many of us, the inability to forgive ourselves was the seed that germinated into service for others."

In some cases, the goal of self-forgiveness is just beyond reach. But Sue's story is proof that two of its ingredients, compassion and empathy, can take root and grow in even the most unlikely of places.

TO MY MOTHER

I was your rebellious son,
do you remember? Sometimes
I wonder if you do remember,
so complete has your forgiveness been.

So complete has your forgiveness been
I wonder sometimes if it did not
precede my wrong, and I erred,
safe found, within your love,

prepared ahead of me, the way home,
or my bed at night, so that almost
I should forgive you, who perhaps
foresaw the worst that I might do.

And forgave before I could act,
causing me to smile now, looking back,
to see how paltry was my worst,
Compared to your forgiveness of it

already given. And this, then,
is the vision of that Heaven of which
we have heard, where those who love
each other have forgiven each other,

where, for that, the leaves are green,
and light a music in the air,
and all is unentangled,
and all is undismayed.

WENDELL BERRY

THE ONLY WAY OUT OF THE LABYRINTH OF SUFFERING IS TO FORGIVE.

JOHN GREEN

"Forgiveness will not be possible until compassion is born in your heart."

THICH NHAT HANH

IT WAS LIKE THIS: YOU WERE HAPPY

It was like this:
you were happy, then you were sad,
then happy again, then not.

It went on.
You were innocent or you were guilty.
Actions were taken, or not.

At times you spoke, at other times you were silent.
Mostly, it seems you were silent—what could you say?

Now it is almost over.

Like a lover, your life bends down and kisses your life.

It does this not in forgiveness—
between you, there is nothing to forgive—

but with the simple nod of a baker at the moment
he sees the bread is finished with transformation.

Eating, too, is a thing now only for others.

It doesn't matter what they will make of you
or your days: they will be wrong,
they will miss the wrong woman, miss the wrong man,
all the stories they tell will be tales of their own invention.

Your story was this: you were happy, then you were sad,
you slept, you awakened.
Sometimes you ate roasted chestnuts, sometimes persimmons.

Jane Hirshfield

"You want to perform a miracle?
Forgive yourself."

RUNE LAZULI

FORGIVENESS IS UNLOCKING THE DOOR TO SET SOMEONE FREE · AND · REALIZING YOU WERE THE PRISONER.

MAX LUCADO

"Forgiveness is a deep process,

which is repeated over and over and over again in our hearts.

It honors the grief and it honors the betrayal.

And in its own time, it ripens into the freedom to truly forgive."

GINA SHARPE

THE DREAM

This has nothing to do with war
or the end of the world. She
dreams there are gray starlings
on the winter lawn and the buds
of next year's oranges alongside
this year's oranges, and the sun
is still up, a watery circle
of fire settling into the sky
at dinner time, but there's no
flame racing through the house
or threatening the bed. When she
wakens the phone is ringing
in a distant room, but she
doesn't go to answer it. No
one is home with her, and the cars
passing before the house hiss
in the rain. "My children!" she
almost says, but there are no
longer children at home, there
are no longer those who would
turn to her, their faces running
with tears, and ask her forgiveness.

PHILIP LEVINE

"IF YOU WANT TO EFFECT CHANGE IN THE
WORLD, IT HAS TO COME THROUGH
NONVIOLENCE AND FORGIVENESS."

WESLEY CLARK JR.

Wesley Clark Jr. and the Ceremony of Forgiveness at Standing Rock

THE SIOUX NATION lived and flourished for centuries on vast areas of unusually rich, fertile land in the area surrounding Standing Rock, North Dakota—a homeland that was taken from them by the American government in the nineteenth century. Just after World War II, the Army Corps of Engineers seized hundreds of thousands of acres from three separate Sioux reservations, and moved its inhabitants onto rocky land where they could no longer feed themselves or make a living. A dam that was constructed on the original land in 1963 has generated $9.6 billion in electrical revenues and $150 million in economic benefit to the surrounding region—none of which reached the tribes from whom the land was stolen.

Throughout the fall of 2016, thousands of Native American "water protectors," as the activists called themselves, along with environmentalists and military veterans, camped together near Cannonball River to defend the sacred Sioux lands against plans to run part of the $3.8 billion, 117-mile Dakota Access Pipeline under a section of the Missouri river near the Standing Rock Sioux Reservation in Fort Yates in North Dakota. After months of protest, the nerves of the activists were growing frayed, and events seemed to be coming to a head. Their best efforts were not bearing fruit. An official order had just been given for the immediate eviction of Oceti Sakowin, the largest of the water protectors' camps. Thousands of veterans were due to arrive in support of the protest the next day. And a blizzard was moving in.

Suddenly, in what felt like a surprise victory, the Army Corps of Engineers announced on December 4 that it would halt any further construction on the pipeline until a more extensive study was completed, the Sioux tribes were consulted, and other routes were considered. On December 5, the day after the reprieve, a group of veterans led by former Army Lieutenant Wesley Clark Jr., son of the former US Army General and NATO commander, came together with leaders of the Sioux Reservation at the Four Prairie Knights Casino Resort at Standing Rock. The veterans had come to North Dakota to join the protest and fully expected to encounter tear gas, rubber bullets, and possibly jail. Instead, they found dancing, singing, and fireworks.

In light of the good news of the previous day, Clark and a group of veterans used the occasion to stand facing a small group of Sioux spiritual leaders in what was soon to be called a "forgiveness ceremony." Wearing the blue uniform of the nineteenth-century Seventh Cavalry, evoking the 140-year-old memory of Lieutenant Colonel George Armstrong Custer, Clark kneeled before the Sioux chief, who placed his hand on Clark's head as Clark asked for forgiveness for centuries of oppression, genocide, and war crimes committed by the US military against tribal nations in this country:

THE WEAK CAN NEVER FORGIVE· FORGIVENESS IS THE ATTRIBUTE OF THE STRONG·

MAHATMA GANDHI

Many of us, me particularly, are from the units that have hurt you over the many years. We came. We fought you. We took your land. We signed treaties that we broke. We stole minerals from your sacred hills. We blasted the faces of our presidents onto your sacred mountain. When we took still more land and then we took your children and then we tried to take your language and we tried to eliminate your language that God gave you, and the Creator gave you. We didn't respect you, we polluted your Earth, we've hurt you in so many ways but we've come to say that we are sorry. We are at your service and we beg for your forgiveness.

With the smoke of ceremonial sage, cedar, and sweetgrass in the air, Chief Leonard Crow Dog, Lakota elder and activist, accepted and—to the amazement of all onlookers—asked, in turn, for forgiveness "for any hurt that might have been caused on June 25, 1876, when the Great Sioux Nation defeated the Seventh Cavalry." He concluded the ceremony by saying, "Let me say a few words of accepting forgiveness: World peace." With hardly a dry eye in the gathering, a loud, unanimous chant began: "World peace!"

In my interview with Wes Clark, we talked about the ways in which the environmental movement has given many people a sense of being related to the larger human family. We are all in this together. We win or lose together. We need to depend on each other to turn crises around and achieve even small victories. As Wes said to me: "Blame twists peoples and societies out of shape. You can't get to peace without forgiveness. There is no moving on without forgiveness." This is remarkable wisdom from one who has served his country in the army, has been to war, and comes from a uniquely distinguished military family.

You can say that nothing tangible came of the forgiveness ceremony at Standing Rock.

No policies were altered. The government has not entertained any notion of reparations to the Sioux people. Most aspects of life in the area have not changed for the better in any dramatic way. And, while some called Clark a hero, many vilified him for taking on the blame for his country.

But every person who stood in that meeting on December 5 was very likely changed in profound ways. Hearts were opened. A new compassion was accessible. There was a sense of all peoples being related. As Wes summed up the day: "If I could live every day of my life like I did that time out there, I'd be the happiest man on Earth."

"The law 'an eye for an eye'
makes the whole world blind."

MAHATMA GANDHI

"Forgiveness is an inner correction

that lightens the heart. It is for our peace of mind first.

Being at peace, we will now have peace to give to others,

and this is the most permanent and valuable gift

we can possibly give."

GERALD JAMPOLSKY

"Real forgiveness means looking steadily at the sin, the sin that is left over without any excuse, after all allowances have been made, and seeing it in all its horror, dirt, meanness and malice, and nevertheless being wholly reconciled to the person who has done it. That, and only that, is forgiveness."

C. S. LEWIS

PLEASE

Forgive me, soldier.
Forgive my right hand
for pointing you
to the flawless
tree line now
outlined in my brain.
There was so much
bloodsky at daybreak
in Pleiku, but I won't say
those infernal guns
blinded me on that hill.

Mistakes piled up men like clouds
pushed to the dark side.
Sometimes I try to retrace
them, running
fingers down the map
telling less than a woman's body—
we followed the grid coordinates

in some battalion commander's mind.
If I could make my mouth
unsay those orders,
I'd holler: Don't
move a muscle. Stay put
keep your fucking head
down, soldier.

Ambush. Gutsmoke.
Last night while making love
I cried out, Hit the dirt!
I've tried to swallow my tongue.
You were a greenhorn, so fearless,
even foolish, & when I said go,
Henry, you went dancing on a red string
of bullets from that tree line
as it moved from a low cloud.

YUSEF KOMUNYAKAA

SWEET MERCY IS NOBILITY'S TRUE BADGE.

WILLIAM SHAKESPEARE,
TITUS ANDRONICUS

"Forgiveness is the key that unlocks the door

of resentment and the handcuffs of hate. It is a power that breaks

the chains of bitterness and the shackles of selfishness."

WILLIAM ARTHUR WARD

THE MEADOW

As we walk into words that have waited for us to enter them, so
the meadow, muddy with dreams, is gathering itself together

and trying, with difficulty, to remember how to make wildflowers.
Imperceptibly heaving with the old impatience, it knows

for certain that two horses walk upon it, weary of hay.
The horses, sway-backed and self-important, cannot design

how the small white pony mysteriously escapes the fence every day.
This is the miracle just beyond their heavy-headed grasp,

and they turn from his nuzzling with irritation. Everything
is crying out. Two crows, rising from the hill, fight

and caw-cry in mid-flight, then fall and light on the meadow grass
bewildered by their weight. A dozen wasps drone, tiny prop planes,

sputtering into a field the farmer has not yet plowed,
and what I thought was a phone, turned down and ringing,

is the knock of a woodpecker for food or warning, I can't say.
I want to add my cry to those who would speak for the sound alone.

But in this world, where something is always listening, even
murmuring has meaning, as in the next room you moan

in your sleep, turning into late morning. My love, this might be
all we know of forgiveness, this small time when you can forget

what you are. There will come a day when the meadow will think
suddenly, water, root, blossom, through no fault of its own,

and the horses will lie down in daisies and clover. Bedeviled,
human, your plight, in waking, is to choose from the words

that even now sleep on your tongue, and to know that tangled
among them and terribly new is the sentence that could change your life.

MARIE HOWE

"The Irish word for forgiveness is *maithiunas*.

It comes from the word *maith*, meaning good. The word is

the same, or similar, in Cymraeg, Gaelg and Gaidhlig—other

languages spoken across the islands of Britain and Ireland.

To forgive someone is 'to good' them. To forgive someone is

to treat them with the goodness with which they did not treat you.

Curiously, this syntax arranges power as the possession of the

troubled one. It is they who can good, and if the one whose hands

caused the trouble asks for forgiveness, they say '*maith dom,*'

'good me.' Forgiveness is not a person, place or thing. Forgiveness,

like priesthood, if it is to be anything, must be a verb."

PÁDRAIG Ó TUAMA

THE FOOT-WASHING

Now you have come,
the roads
humbling your feet with dust:

I ask you to
sit by this
spring:

I will wash your feet
with springwater
and silver care:

I lift leaking handbowls
to your ankles:
O ablutions!

Who are you
sir
who are my brother?

I dry your feet
with sweetgum
and mintleaves:

the odor of your feet
is newly earthen,
honeysuckled:

bloodwork in blue
raisures over the white
skinny anklebone:

if I have wronged you
cleanse me with the falling
water of forgiveness.

And woman, your flat feet
yellow, gray with dust,
your orphaned udders flat,

lift your dress
up to your knees
and I will wash your feet:

feel the serenity
cool as cool springwater
and hard to find:

if I have failed to know
the grief in your gone time,
forgive me wakened now.

A. R. AMMONS

Forgiveness at the End of Life

A Conversation with Koshin Paley Ellison and Robert Chodo Campbell

EXPERIENCING the end of life, while knowing that it is in fact the end, can be a profoundly rich experience, despite its inevitable sadness and fear. Whether or not one consciously enters into a life-review process, most people seem intuitively drawn to examining their past, their greatest pleasures, and often their deepest pains and regrets. For many, the issue of forgiveness—whether offering or asking for it—can become a defining issue of this time.

Koshin and Chodo, cofounders of New York's Zen Center for Contemplative Care, have spent years helping people who are confronting illness and approaching death. Koshin is the editor of the groundbreaking book *Awake at the Bedside: Contemplative*

Teachings on Palliative and End-of-Life Care, a collection of offerings from uniquely experienced and wise authors on the subject. They affirmed for me that pondering forgiveness at this delicate time in one's life can take many different forms. They have chosen to bring their experience to a course they regularly teach at their Center asking participants to pretend they have only nine months to live.

Some are eager to bring closure where there has been a painful rift. For others, denying forgiveness at the end can be a way to exert a sense of final control over an uncontrollable situation. Others are eager to ease the burden of a heavy heart that has been tightly holding onto blaming and grudges. Still others find offering forgiveness proof of their own authenticity. And some struggle with the question, "Who will I be if I let go of this anger that has defined me for so long?"

Along the path to forgiveness, it seems a relief to many to be reminded that forgiveness is not forgetting. It is not denying what happened. The original offense does not disappear, and no reconciliation is necessary. But, with an open and compassionate heart, one can see the offender as someone who—like everyone else—is simply an imperfect human being. Forgiveness means standing in a different place as regards the person or incident that caused the pain. Those who are able to bring forgiveness into their lives at the end most often experience it as profound freedom and release, accompanied by a new lightness of heart.

Koshin and Chodo told me three people's stories of grappling with forgiveness at the end.

A much-beloved grandmother living in hospice in her final weeks always seemed to have a flood of visitors, many of whom came to ask her forgiveness for slights and disappointments that they had committed toward her over the years. She unhesitatingly granted their wishes, enjoying the relief in the eyes of her visitors. Koshin remarked

AS LONG AS THE CANDLE BURNS, THERE IS TIME TO MAKE REPAIRS.

RABBI SALANTER

that the issue of forgiveness was not at the core of this wish-granting. Instead, she was determined to, as he said, "live in grace," and giving her visitors a sense of happy resolution was what nurtured her.

A woman who had sacrificed her own life in order to care for two invalid parents for over twenty years was freed after their death to finally create and engage in her own life. At that juncture, her husband left her. Then she was diagnosed with advanced metastatic cancer. As she confronted her impending death, her decades of accumulated rage found a channel for release. She screamed and spewed venom at all her nurses, caregivers, and visitors. Koshin was asked to visit her in the hope of easing her end-of-life process. On his first visit, she threw things at him, berated him, and ordered him to go away. Instead, he pulled up a chair and listened to the ongoing diatribe with a loving and accepting heart—saying nothing, just listening. He was never able to witness any great mellowing that he had hoped might surface at the end. Instead, at her moment of death, she raised her arms in a final, defiant scream, raging against the blows that life had dealt her. Her screams, after decades of repressed anger, were, in a sense, her offering of forgiveness to herself. As David Whyte has written: "Anger is the deepest form of compassion, for another, for the world, for the self, for a life, for the body, for a family and for all our ideals, all vulnerable and all, possibly about to be hurt."

Koshin was called in to visit a man living in hospice who had one dying wish. More than anything, the man wanted to see his daughter, from whom he had been estranged for many years. She refused to see or speak with him, as her father had caused great pain in her life. Koshin called her three times on behalf of her father before she at last agreed to come to her father's bedside and he was able to ask for her forgiveness. She not only angrily refused his wish but let loose an enraged diatribe against the father she felt had so deeply wronged and wounded her, ending with the final shout, "I hate you!"

"The bitterest tears shed over graves are for words left unsaid and deeds left undone."

HARRIET BEECHER STOWE

The father had the wisdom to see this exchange as exactly what his daughter needed—"my final gift to her." As Koshin remarked in telling this story, "Forgiveness is not always sweet."

While there are no formulas for bringing forgiveness into the end of life, most agree that, as Stephen and Ondrea Levine write, "Those who forgive the most profoundly seem to heal the deepest. Love is a gatekeeper that, unlike most, struggles to keep the gate open."

Many who work with the dying offer four phrases as a kind of mantra that, when repeated over and over, can open the heart to forgiveness:

Please forgive me.

I forgive you.

Thank you.

I love you.

FORGIVENESS JUST ONCE

forgiveness just once
i asked one time
so my retribution go unpaided

but life just laughed
and said don't ask
for the debt is yours selfmaded

SHAUN SHANE

"To carry a grudge is like being stung to death by one bee."

WILLIAM H. WALTON

LIFE
IS AN ADVENTURE
IN FORGIVENESS.

NORMAN COUSINS

UNDER ONE SMALL STAR

My apologies to chance for calling it necessity.

My apologies to necessity if I'm mistaken, after all.

Please, don't be angry, happiness, that I take you as my due.

May my dead be patient with the way my memories fade.

My apologies to time for all the world I overlook each second.

My apologies to past loves for thinking that the latest is the first.

Forgive me, open wounds, for pricking my finger.

I apologize for my record of minutes to those who cry from
the depths.

I apologize to those who wait in railway stations for being asleep
today at five a.m.

Pardon me, hounded hope, for laughing from time to time.

Pardon me, deserts, that I don't rush to you bearing a spoonful
of water.

And you, falcon, unchanging year after year, always in the
same cage,

your gaze always fixed on the same point in space,

forgive me, even if it turns out you were stuffed.

My apologies to the felled tree for the table's four legs.

My apologies to great questions for small answers.

Truth, please don't pay me much attention.

Dignity, please be magnanimous.

Bear with me, O mystery of existence, as I pluck the occasional thread from your train.

Soul, don't take offense that I've only got you now and then.

My apologies to everything that I can't be everywhere at once.

My apologies to everyone that I can't be each woman and each man.

I know I won't be justified as long as I live,

since I myself stand in my own way.

Don't bear me ill will, speech, that I borrow weighty words, then labor heavily so that they may seem light.

WISŁAWA SZYMBORSKA

"If little faults proceeding on distemper

Shall not be winked at, how shall we stretch our eye

When capital crimes, chewed, swallowed,

And digested,

Appear before us?"

WILLIAM SHAKESPEARE, *HENRY V*

ONE OF THE SECRETS OF A LONG

AND FRUITFUL LIFE IS TO FORGIVE

EVERYBODY

EVERYTHING

EVERY NIGHT

BEFORE YOU GO TO BED.

BERNARD BARUCH

A RECKONING

At my age, one begins
To chalk up all his sins,
Hoping to wipe the slate
Before it is too late.

Therefore I call to mind
All memories of the kind
That make me wince and sweat
And tremble with regret.

What do these prove to be?
In every one, I see
Shocked faces, that, alas,
Now know me for an ass.

Fatuities that I
Have uttered, drunk or dry,
Return now in a rush
And make my old cheek blush.

But how can I repent
From mere embarrassment?
Damn-foolishness can't well
Entitle me to Hell.

Well, I shall put the blame
On the pride that's in my shame.
Of that I must be shriven
If I'm to be forgiven.

RICHARD WILBUR

"There is a hard law:

when a deep injury is done to us,

we never recover until we forgive."

ALAN PATON

"A wise man will make haste to forgive,

because he knows the true value of time, and will not

suffer it to pass away in unnecessary pain."

SAMUEL JOHNSON

LO, NOW, MY GUEST

Lo, now my guest, if aught amiss were said,

Forgive it and dismiss it from your head.

For me, for you, for all, to close the date,

Pass now the ev'ning sponge across the slate;

And to that spirit of forgiveness keep

Which is the parent and the child of sleep.

ROBERT LOUIS STEVENSON

A BUDDHIST PRAYER OF FORGIVENESS

If I have harmed anyone in any way either knowingly or unknowingly through my own confusions I ask their forgiveness.

If anyone has harmed me in any way either knowingly or unknowingly through their own confusions I forgive them.

If there is a situation I am not yet ready to forgive I forgive myself for that.

For all the ways that I harm myself, negate, doubt, belittle myself, judge or be unkind to myself through my own confusions I forgive myself.

THIS IS JUST TO SAY

I have eaten

the plums

that were in

the icebox

and which

you were probably

saving

for breakfast

Forgive me

they were delicious

so sweet

and so cold

WILLIAM CARLOS WILLIAMS

Acknowledgments

Heartfelt thanks go to the amazing team at Wisdom Publications, especially executive editor Josh Bartok, CEO/publisher Daniel Aitken, and chairperson of Wisdom's board Tim McNeill. Several years ago, they took a chance on this unknown, first-time author. I hope that the journey we have taken together through three books has proven them good risk-takers.

Learning that I was working on a book on forgiveness, armies of both friends and strangers stepped forward with stories of their own, beautiful poetry and invaluable introductions and connections. Stories of forgiveness are often painfully personal, even heartbreaking, and I am deeply indebted to those who wanted to share them with me. They were my true teachers in this exploration.

Boundless gratitude for all manner of guidance and inspiration go to more wonderful people than I can list here. Beloved Buddhist teacher and writer Jack Kornfield's many wise and generous works on forgiveness set the bar extraordinarily high indeed for any further explorations of the subject. Sharon Salzberg has written eloquently on forgiveness and offered many moving meditations to increase its power in our lives. As always, I am indebted to Joseph Goldstein's many writings and dharma talks that awaken forgiveness in beautiful ways. Religious leaders and other teachers include His Holiness the Dalai Lama, Desmond Tutu, Thich Nhat Hanh, Zen monks Koshin Paley Ellison and Robert Chodo Campbell, Pádraig Ó Tuama, Islamic scholar Dr. Celene Ibrahim, and Rabbis Jodie Gordon and Neil Hirsch. As with all my work, the contributions to my understanding from friend/teacher/mentor Mu Soeng have been invaluable. The work of Dr. Robert Enright, founder of the International Forgiveness Institute, and Dr. Fred Luskin of the Stanford University Forgiveness Project has been seminal to my understanding. Among many others, Helice and Steve Picheny, Smitty Pignatelli and Allyce Najimy, Edith Velmans, Stephen Cope, Michael Lipson, Eve Shatz, Hannah Toffey Peters, Peter Greer, and the great poet Marie Howe have provided invaluable suggestions and inspirations.

Additionally, I am indebted to many of the subjects of the profiles in the book, particularly Will Morales, Wes Clark, Congressman John Lewis, Brenda Jones, and Sue Klebold. The list is embarrassingly incomplete, and if your name is not here please know that its absence is only a reflection of my mental lapses in recollecting every step along this long path.

As with my first two books, not a page would have come out nearly as well without the brilliance of Tresca Weinstein, writing partner and editor extraordinaire, who not only kept me out of trouble but also made the book sing. And, once again, Rob Forman suggested some of the best poems in the book.

There would have been nothing at all to edit without the lifelong cheerleading of Alexandra and Charlie Socarides, the true inspirations in my life.

Poetry Permissions

Index of Names and Sources

About the Author

Barbara Bonner has spent her professional life devoted to nonprofit leadership, fundraising, and philanthropy. Originally an art historian specializing in seventeenth-century European painting, Barbara went on to hold leadership positions in three of New York's distinguished museums. She then served as vice president of Bennington College and later of the Kripalu Center for Yoga and Health. For many years she has had her own consulting practice that helps nonprofit organizations reach new levels of prosperity and thriving. Barbara has also held leadership positions on ten nonprofit boards, most recently as chair of the board of The Barre Center for Buddhist Studies. Five years ago she started a fund for women with cancer in Berkshire County, Massachusetts.

Her first book, *Inspiring Generosity*, was published by Wisdom Publications in 2014, followed by *Inspiring Courage* in 2017. *Inspiring Forgiveness* is the third in the series.

Barbara lives in the beautiful Berkshire hills of western Massachusetts in a converted barn. She is an avid reader, gardener, swimmer, and perpetual student of yoga and meditation. Buddhist study and practice are at the center of her life. She is currently embarked on meditation teacher training with Jack Kornfield and Tara Brach.

For more details you can visit www.barbarabonner.org.

What to Read Next from Wisdom Publications

Inspiring Generosity

Barbara Bonner

"This book is a great act of generosity on Barbara Bonner's part, opening your hand, your heart, and your life in new and unexpected ways. Read it and you will love it!"
—Robert A. F. Thurman, Columbia University

Inspiring Courage

Barbara Bonner

"*Inspiring Courage* touches the heart and fills you with spirit."
—Jack Kornfield, author of *A Path with Heart*

Daily Doses of Wisdom
A Year of Buddhist Inspiration
Edited by Josh Bartok

"Directions: Read one page a day. Can be taken with meal. Side effects may include insight, compassion, and wisdom. Stop immediately if experiencing nirvana."
—Sumi Loundon, author of *Blue Jean Buddha*

The Poetry of Mindfulness, Impermanence, and Joy
Edited by John Brehm

"This collection would make a lovely gift for a poetry-loving or dharma-practicing friend, it could also serve as a wonderful gateway to either topic for the uninitiated."
—*Tricycle: The Buddhist Review*

About Wisdom Publications

Wisdom Publications is the leading publisher of classic and contemporary Buddhist books and practical works on mindfulness. To learn more about us or to explore our other books, please visit our website at wisdomexperience.org or contact us at the address below.

Wisdom Publications
199 Elm Street
Somerville, MA 02144 USA

We are a 501(c)(3) organization, and donations in support of our mission are tax deductible.

Wisdom Publications is affiliated with the Foundation for the Preservation of the Mahayana Tradition (FPMT).